CULTURES OF THE WORLD

Nepal

Cavendish
Square
New York

Published in 2014 by Cavendish Square Publishing, LLC
303 Park Avenue South, Suite 1247, New York, NY 10010

Third Edition

This publication is published with arrangement with Marshall Cavendish International (Asia) Pte Ltd.

Copyright © 2014 Marshall Cavendish International (Asia) Pte Ltd.

Website: cavendishsq.com

Cultures of the World is a registered trademark of Times Publishing Limited.

This publication represents the opinions and views of the author based on his or her personal experience, knowledge, and research. The information in this book serves as a general guide only. The author and publisher have used their best efforts in preparing this book and disclaim liability rising directly or indirectly from the use and application of this book.

CPSIA Compliance Information: Batch #WW14CSQ

All websites were available and accurate when this book was sent to press.

Library of Congress Cataloging-in-Publication Data
Burbank, Jon.
Nepal / by Jon Burbank and Josie Elias.
 p. cm. — (Cultures of the world)
Includes bibliographical references and index.
ISBN 978-0-76148-013-6 (hardcover) ISBN 978-1-62712-624-3 (paperback) ISBN 978-0-76148-021-1 (ebook)
1. Nepal — Juvenile literature. I. Burbank, Jon, 1951-. II. Title.
DS493.4 .B87 2014
954.96—d23

Writers: Jon Burbank and Josie Elias
Editor: Mindy Pang
Designer: Adithi

PICTURE CREDITS
Cover: © Jacek Kadaj / Alamy
Audrius Tomonis – www.banknotes.com: 135 • Corbis / Click Photos: 29, 47, 61, 62, 115, 118, 120, 121, 123, 125, 126 • Getty Images: 30, 57, 94, 95, 106, 111, 112 • Inmagine.com / Alamy: 1, 3, 5, 6, 7, 8, 9, 10, 11, 13, 14, 15, 16, 17, 18, 19, 22, 23, 25, 28, 34, 35, 36, 37, 39, 40, 42, 43, 45, 46, 48, 49, 50, 51, 52, 53, 54, 55, 56, 58, 59, 60, 63, 64, 65, 66, 67, 68, 69, 71, 72, 73, 74, 76, 77, 78, 79, 80, 81, 82, 83, 84, 85, 86, 87, 88, 89, 90, 91, 92, 93, 96, 97, 98, 99, 100, 101, 102 (bottom), 104, 105, 107, 108, 109, 110, 116, 117, 119, 122, 124, 127, 128, 129, 130, 131 • Marshall Cavendish Archives: 12, 20, 70, 75, 102 (top) • Reuters: 113, 114 • Wikimedia Commons: 24, 26, 27

PRECEDING PAGE
The view over Namche Bazaar to Thamserku mountain in Sagarmatha National Park.

Printed in the United States of America

CONTENTS

NEPAL TODAY

MOST PEOPLE KNOW NEPAL AS THE HOME OF MOUNT EVEREST, the world's tallest mountain. The Himalaya is the world's highest mountain range that stretches across Nepal's northern border and includes eight of the 10 tallest mountains in the world. The country is mountainous, hilly, landlocked, and about the same size as the state of Arkansas. Nepal has enormous physical diversity, especially for a relatively small country. It is commonly divided into three geographic regions: the mountain, the hill, and the Terai, which is the northern rim of the Gangetic Plain at about 196 feet (60 m). The lifestyle of the people living within each region is largely dictated by the climatic conditions of the area that are determined by altitude.

Nepal is world famous for its spectacular mountain scenery and it also boasts a rich architectural history. The capital, Kathmandu, is the commercial, political, and cultural center of Nepal. It is a fascinating and exotic showcase of a very rich and diverse culture. The Kathmandu Valley is the main area of hill settlement in Nepal and is home to a concentration of monuments that are inscribed on the United Nations World Heritage List. The monuments and buildings include the Durbar Squares of

A Tibetan monastery in Nepal.

Hanuman Dhoka (Kathmandu), Patan, and Bhaktapur, the Buddhist stupas of Swayambhu and Boudhanath, and the Hindu temples of Pashupati and Changu Narayan.

Hinduism and Buddhism are the two major religions practiced in Nepal, with the majority of the people being Hindus. These two religions have coexisted for hundreds of years. Many Buddhist shrines house Hindu idols. Some gods and goddesses are revered in Hinduism and Buddhism although they have different names. Buddhists worship at some Hindu temples and Hindus worship at some Buddhist shrines without a second thought as many people worship in both. Other religions such as Islam, Christianity, Jainism, Sikhism, and Bon are also practiced in Nepal. Tharus practice animism and the Kirants, who are the earliest inhabitants of the country, practice their own kind of religion based on ancestor worship. These religions have influenced each other over the years so that some ideas and beliefs have been combined and incorporated. In 2006, after the abolition of the monarchy, Nepal was declared a secular country where previously it had been the only Hindu kingdom in the world.

Nepal's population is made up of dozens of different ethnic groups and 124 different languages are spoken. Some of the main ethnic groups are: Newars who live in and around the Kathmandu Valley; Sherpas and Lopas who live in the mountain regions; Tharus and Yadavis who live in the Terai; and Brahmins, Chhetris, and Thakuris who live in most parts of the country. Nepali is the official language of the state, spoken and understood by most of the people. English is spoken in some government offices and businesses. Most Nepalese speak their mother tongue and Nepali, and many speak another language as well.

The population of Nepal is just more than 30 million, and the city of Kathmandu has a population of just more than 1 million. More than half of the total population of the country live in the Terai region followed by the Hill and Mountain regions that constitutes about 43 and 7 percent, respectively. The urban population of Nepal is about 17 percent compared with a rural population of 83 percent.

It is surprising to know that the air quality in Kathmandu is very poor. Air pollution is normally associated with very large, densely populated, and industrialized cities. Kathmandu does not have many large industries and compared with the population density of other cities around the world it is not even very big. But more than 85 percent of the country's energy needs are met by traditional solid fuels: firewood, agricultural residues, and animal waste. In recent years there has been an increase in the number of people in Nepal suffering from chronic pulmonary obstructive disease that is caused by burning of wood and cow-dung cake and pollution from industries and vehicles. The increase in the number of diesel vehicles in Kathmandu is a major cause of air pollution. To combat this there have been initiatives to introduce electric vehicles that have zero emissions for both private and public transportation. Solar power is being introduced to replace firewood as an energy source.

A busy street in Banepa.

Water pollution is also an issue because the rivers are used as dumping grounds. Solar Powered Ozone Water Treatment Systems (SPOWTS) have been developed and introduced. They are designed specifically to purify water in holding tanks and make it safe and potable. SPOWTS also allows villagers to sell clean water to tourists and trekkers without the need for plastic water bottles that are not biodegradable and have added to the pollution problem. Issues of air and water pollution are being addressed in the Kathmandu Valley, but in the rural areas, where most of the people live, it has been more difficult to address the issues because of inaccessibility. Incidence of acute respiratory tract infection and diarrheal diseases continues to be high. Although new

A Nepali shepherd carries two baby goats in Jagat, located in the Manaslu region.

roads are being built, traditionally people in Nepal walk, and they carry whatever needs to be transported with them. To see a man walking along and carrying a refrigerator or a huge quantity of firewood on his back is not unusual. The lack of infrastructure makes it harder for foreign aid and initiatives to reach the remote areas.

Nepal is one of the least developed countries in the world. The majority of the population depends on agriculture for their livelihood. Tourism, one of the main sources of income in the past, has been affected adversely due to civil conflict and violence. This has had an impact on the standard of living of those people dependent on tourism both in Kathmandu and in rural areas. Tour and trekking operators have seen their business drop off dramatically following strikes in May 2012. It was estimated that 40 percent of tours were cancelled, mostly booked by potential visitors from Europe and India. Hotels have seen a downturn in their bookings, combined with cancellations of holidays already booked. Pavitra Kumar Karki, President of the Nepal Association of Tour and Travel Agents (NATTA), stated that travelers need to feel confident when booking their holidays, and that even the government is seen to be helpless to ensure their safety.

Political instability and civil unrest have been a problem in Nepal for many years and have resulted in the overthrow of the monarchy and constant upheavals within government. The 10-year Maoist insurgency was resolved in 2006 by bringing the Maoists into the political mainstream. Writing the new constitution was supposed to bring an end to the interim period during which details of Nepal's democracy were supposed to be written in to a new constitution. The political situation in Nepal remains fragile.

Illegal road blocks and strikes occur, often without notice, resulting in the closure of businesses and vehicles not being allowed to move on the roads. Crimes such as assault, theft, and violent demonstrations have recently occurred in the Terai, resulting in injuries and deaths. There have been violent incidents and bomb attacks at crowded locations and on public transportation throughout the country. On April 30, 2012, a bomb attack during a protest in Janakpur injured many and killed four people. On February 27, 2012, a petrol bomb exploded in front of the Nepal Oil Corporation's Central Office in Kathmandu, killing three people and injuring others. Four explosive devices were detonated on buses in the western Terai region in 2011, killing one person and injuring almost 50 others.

Most of the violence, strikes, and disharmony can be attributed to political groups attempting to gain the upper hand in forthcoming elections. Strikes and violent clashes between security forces and demonstrators at unprecedented levels have occurred in recent months after lawmakers failed to agree on a new constitution in May 2012, leaving the country with no legal government. Riot police patrolled the streets and security forces were on alert after several political parties called for rallies to demand the resignation of Prime Minister Baburam Bhattarai and to protest his unilateral decision to call for elections in November 2012. Unfortunately, the elections have since been further delayed to November 2013 due to disagreements among political parties and unability to promulgate the constitution.

Living on mountain sides and in narrow valleys, speaking different languages, and worshipping different gods, somehow the dozens of ethnic groups in Nepal had lived together for years in peace. Much of the ongoing debate now is whether to draw state boundaries in a way that will boost the power of the country's ethnic minorities. As Nepal struggles to create a new government some politicians are insisting that the marginalized communities deserve to live in states that maximize their influence. Other politicians are opposed to states drawn along ethnic and caste lines. With the elections in November 2013 it is to be hoped that a solution may finally be reached that will lead to harmony and progress in the country again. Although Nepal is ranked as one of the poorest and least developed countries in the world, its mix of ancient cultures and awe-inspiring physical beauty makes it one of the world's richest and most fascinating places on the earth.

Many goods are transported through hills on the rugged backs of the Sherpa porters. Developments comes slowly due to the lack of roads, electricity, and other necessities.

GEOGRAPHY

The Marsyangdi river valley is part of the Annapurna Conservation Area in Gandaki. Nepal is home to the Himalayas, the tallest and youngest mountain range in the world.

1

MILLIONS OF YEARS AGO, the earth had only one immense land mass, which scientists have called Pangaea. Eventually this supercontinent broke up, and, over time, the pieces moved apart and then recombined in different ways until they began to resemble the continents we recognize today. This movement of tectonic plates is ongoing and continues to cause geographic changes.

Nepal is one of the richest countries in the world in terms of biodiversity due to its geographical location. Although landlocked, its elevation starts at 196 feet (60 m) above sea level and rises to the highest point on earth, the summit of Mount Everest, at 29,034 feet (8,850 m). Within these elevations climatic conditions range from subtropical to arctic and result in an enormous variety of ecosystems.

The village of Jharkot lies in the midst of the Nepalese Himalayas. Along trade routes in the mountains, caravans and horses are used to transport goods from one town to another. The steep and rugged geography of Nepal makes it difficult and impractical to build roads.

Nepal's story began about 10 to 15 million years ago when present-day India was a separate continent, not attached to Asia but slowly moving toward it. When the two land masses finally collided, the pressure that resulted pushed the edges of the two continents up, forming majestic mountains and a series of hills below the mountains. Thus Nepal was born.

Nepal is a landlocked country, surrounded by Tibet and China in the north and India in the south. It has an area of 56,827 square miles (147,181 square km) with a population of 30.4 million people.

Although 85 percent of Nepal is mountainous, the country can be divided into three geographic regions: the towering Himalaya mountain range, the cool terraces and valleys that form the Middle Hills, and the warm, humid lowlands of the Terai (teh-RYE).

THE HIMALAYA

Himalaya comes from two words in Sanskrit, one of the oldest languages in the world. *Hima* means "snow" and *alaya* means "abode." This is not surprising as the mountain peaks are covered with snow throughout the year. The Himalaya consists of a collection of huge mountain ranges that extend beyond Nepal across Bhutan in the east and into Pakistan in the west.

The subcontinent of India used to be part of southern Africa, Australia, and Antarctica. The movement of the earth's crust over millions of years pushed these lands apart, and India fused with the Asian continent.

MOUNT EVEREST

Worldwide there are only 14 mountain peaks more than 26,247 feet (8,000 m). Eight of the 10 tallest mountains above sea level are in Nepal, including Mount Everest, the tallest at 29,035 feet (8,850 m).

Despite numerous attempts, no climbers scaled Mount Everest until Sir Edmund Hillary and Tenzing Norgay, a Sherpa guide, finally reached the top in 1953. In 1978 Reinhold Messner and his partner Peter Habler were the first to climb it without using bottled oxygen.

At different times, other mountain peaks were thought to hold the title of highest in the world. Dhaulagiri, Kangchenjunga, and Gauri Shankar (visible from the Kathmandu Valley) were all once thought to hold the crown.

In 1863, when India was ruled by Great Britain, a survey done by the Indian Survey Office confirmed Everest as the tallest mountain in the world. On the Tibetan side, Everest is called Chomolungma and on the Nepali side Sagarmatha. Both names mean "mother of the world." The surveyors, unaware of these names, first called it Peak 15, and then Everest, after a former head of the survey office.

In the mid-1980s Everest's position as the tallest mountain in the world was challenged when a geographer claimed that Mount K2 in Pakistan was taller, but measurements using laser and satellite technology confirmed Everest as the tallest. This was confirmed in 1999 by two American climbers supported by five Sherpa guides.

A typical village in the lower middle hills along the Manaslu trail. Terraced fields have been carved out of the hillsides for growing rice, barley, beans, and millet.

The altitude of the snow line depends on precipitation but is normally around 16,500 feet (5,029 m). Permanent settlements such as Khumjung are found up to about 12,400 feet (3,780 m). Seasonal encampments are located at higher altitudes. Settlements catering for trekkers are located at around 15,700 feet (4685 m). Above 19,500 feet (5,943 m) the region is considered an arctic desert.

About 43 percent of Nepal's land is at altitudes of more than 10,000 feet (3,048 m). Almost 7 percent of the population lives at these elevations, working as traders, herders, and farmers. Barley, millet, and potatoes are among the few crops that can grow at altitudes of up to 14,000 feet (4,267 m).

THE MIDDLE HILLS

Ask people in the Middle Hills traveling to Kathmandu where they are going, and chances are the answer will be "Nepal." For many, Kathmandu is Nepal.

Half of Nepal lies in an area called the Mahabharat Range, or the Middle Hills, and just under 50 percent of the population lives here. The height of these hills varies from 5,000 to 12,000 feet (1,524—3,658 m), so calling them "hills" is a little misleading, because almost anywhere else in the world they would be called mountains. Mount Kosciusko, the highest mountain in Australia, is 7,310 feet (2,228 m) tall.

Seen from the air, the Middle Hills resemble a series of endless steep ridges. Over the centuries, the Nepalese have built steep terraces on these hills to grow food.

THE KATHMANDU VALLEY

The Kathmandu Valley has always been the heart of Nepal. Although only about 450 square miles (1,166 square km) in land area, it is home to 2.5 million people. The valley lies at an elevation of 4,383 feet (1,336 m), which gives it a mild climate. Temperatures rarely go above 86°F (30°C) in the hot season, and in winter the temperature rarely falls below 32°F (0°C).

The capital city of Kathmandu has a population of more than 1 million people. It was founded by King Gunakamadeva in the eighth century. Kath *means "wood" and* mandir *means "temple" or "edifice." The name Kathmandu was derived from a wooden temple built in the 10th century that still stands in the central square.*

Kathmandu's rapid growth has caused serious environmental problems. The air quality in the city is considered among the worst in the world, and there is a severe shortage of clean water. Garbage and industrial waste also threaten the environment.

The rugged landscape makes it near impossible to build roads, so Nepalese usually travel on foot. Distances are not measured in miles, but in hours or days it takes to walk to a destination. Men, women, and children all carry food, school books, and medical supplies on their backs to their destinations.

Nearly 32 percent of forest cover occurs in the Middle Hills, but the area, once crowned with thick, luxuriant forests, is becoming more and more barren. Villagers depend on the forests for fodder, firewood, and building

People and animals on farmland in Bardia. Most of Nepal's rice is grown in the Terai region. Few machines are used for farming. Instead, animals are often used to plow the land.

materials. As the population increases, trees are being cut faster than they can be replaced. Unfortunately, the loss of foliage causes village water supplies to dry up, and soil erosion eats away at the hillsides.

There are several large valleys scattered among the hills. The largest one is the Pokhara Valley in central Nepal. The most famous valley, however, is Kathmandu Valley, 124 miles (200 km) east of Pokhara.

THE TERAI

Nepal's only flat area is a narrow strip along the southern border with India. This strip called the Terai is less than 1,000 feet (304.8 m) above sea level. Because it forms part of the flood plain of the Ganges River in northern India, the Terai is very fertile.

The Terai used to be covered with thick jungle and was uninhabitable because of malaria, a disease spread by mosquitoes. In the 1950s the World Health Organization (WHO) sponsored a program to spray large tracts of the Terai with the pesticide DDT. The malaria was brought under control, and hill people began to settle in the area. The Terai quickly changed into Nepal's bread basket and rice bowl. It is also the center for what little industry Nepal has.

Today, the Terai is home to 50.2 percent of the population. Every year, people from the Middle Hills migrate here at an increasing rate.

The climate of the Terai is extremely hot, with temperatures in the summer (April—June) reaching 100°F (38°C). A deadly wind called the *loo* (loo), with temperatures of more than 113°F (45°C), sometimes kills people in the fields. The heavy monsoon rains from June to September bring cooler temperatures and rain to the rice fields.

RIVERS

Nepal has thousands of streams, which flow down mountains and hillsides into hundreds of rivers. Yet out of those hundreds of rivers, or *bhote* (BOH-tay) in Nepalese, only three are strong enough to cut through the Middle Hills down to the Terai and on to the dusty plains of India. These three rivers are the Kosi in the east, the Kali in the center, and the Karnali in the west.

During the monsoon, the heavy rains cause the rivers to overflow. There are few bridges in Nepal, and most are washed away yearly by flood waters. Flooding rivers can sweep away houses and even whole villages. All of Nepal's rivers flow across the Gangetic plain and drain into the Ganges. The floods that frequently devastate Nepal also cause devastation in India.

The rivers have tremendous hydroelectric potential, but building and maintaining hydroelectric plants in Nepal's rugged landscape would be difficult and expensive. The cost of the electricity produced would be so high that most Nepalese would not be able to afford electricity. Projects where a small hydroelectric plant provides electricity for a small village have proven more effective.

A bridge sits over a river in Nepal. Snow from the mountains feed Nepal's rivers and streams.

FLORA

The extremes of altitude in Nepal create a variety of climates and environments that support a fascinating variety of plants. There are approximately 6,500 species of flowering plants and ferns, 300 of which are endemic to Nepal.

The Terai has been identified as the region with the greatest economic potential for the forest sector in Nepal. Teak (*Tectona grandis*) is one of the dominant tree species in this area. A hardwood species called Sal (*Shorea robusta*) grows in the natural forests of the tropical moist lowland Indo-Malayan forests below altitudes of 3,280 feet (1,000 m). Sal provides excellent timber for building homes and furniture. A species of mimosa, *Acacia catechu*, replaces Sal in the riverine forests. The bark of this tree is astringent and has a large amount of antioxidant, anti-inflammatory, antibacterial, and antifungal properties. It is used as a herbal medicine to treat high blood pressure, dysentery, and bronchitis.

In the Middle Hills, there are pines, alders, oaks, hemlock, birches, and forests of evergreens such as juniper. There are also many forests of large rhododendron trees in the east and center of the country.

The bright red rhododendron blossom is Nepal's national flower. Entire hillsides turn red in the spring when the rhododendron forests bloom; this is one of Nepal's most beautiful sights.

A rhododendron blossom forest along Annapurna. The rhododendron is the national flower of Nepal. These trees can be found at altitudes up to 9,000 feet (2,743 m).

Nepal's forests provide more than 35 percent of all the energy used in the country. Forests are also a major source of animal fodder and timber for construction. Deforestation has caused severe environmental degradation and soil erosion. One report says 3 percent of Nepal's forests are disappearing every year. Once a section of hillside is logged, the monsoon rains wash away the topsoil into the rivers, which eventually carry it as far as the Bay of Bengal. Without this fertile soil, nothing can grow on the hills.

The Nepalese government is working with foreign aid agencies to foster community forestry projects. Each village is responsible for replenishing its own forest by growing tree nurseries. Still, it takes a generation to replace what is cut down in a few minutes.

ANIMAL LIFE

Bengal tiger (*Panthera tigris*), greater one-horned rhinoceros (*Rhinoceros unicornis*), Asian elephant (*Elephas maximus*), spotted deer (*Axis axis*), swamp deer (*Cervus duvauceli*), gaur (*Bos gaurus*), monkeys, and all kinds of smaller mammals dwell in the jungles of the lowlands, especially in the national parks. The gaur is the largest wild cattle species in the world weighing up to 2000 lbs.

THE YETI

Nepal's most famous resident, the yeti (also called the Abominable Snowman), may not exist at all. The Sherpas, who share its habitat, call it the "yet-tch" and have even distinguished two different types: one that eats cattle and another that eats people.

The yeti was dismissed as a legend until a British army major, L.A. Waddell, found huge footprints in the snow in 1889. In 1921 the leader of an Everest expedition reported seeing a dark creature walking in the snow and found some strange footprints.

The yeti has managed to elude discovery despite numerous expeditions sent to capture it. The famous mountain climber Eric Shipton found a set of footprints in 1951 that prompted several expeditions, including one led by Sir Edmund Hillary, the first conqueror of Everest.

Interest in the yeti died down after a series of disappointments. A supposed yeti scalp was taken from the Pangboche Monastery for tests and identified as belonging to a mountain goat. Most of the pictures of yeti footprints were found to be small bird and rodent tracks that had melted in the sun.

Interest rose again in 1974 when a Sherpa woman was allegedly attacked by a yeti, who also killed several of her yaks.

What does a yeti look like? Tall, perhaps taller than a person, with orange fur, and a pointed head. Some reports say its feet point backward. One theory claims that it belongs to a species of giant orangutans that was thought extinct. Until one is actually found, however, the identity of the yeti will remain a mystery.

(900 kg). Nepal has also two species of crocodiles: gharials (*Gavialis gangeticus*) have a needle-shaped snout and eat mostly fish and muggers (*Crocodylus palustris*) have big snouts, and can grow up to 10 feet (3.5 m) long.

Nepal's most reclusive resident is the rare snow leopard (*Uncia uncia*). Little was known about this beautiful silver and black cat until recently. They live in the high Himalayan region. It is estimated that there are less than 500 snow leopards in Nepal, but this is approximately a tenth of the world's known snow leopard population. They are opportunistic predators and known to kill sheep, goats, horses, and yak calves. The snow-leopard-human conflict is one of the main threats to its survival. They are also threatened by poaching and habitat degradation.

There are ongoing conservation programs to rebuild the populations of tigers, rhinoceros, snow leopards, and gharials, which are all threatened with extinction. Not everyone, however, is in favor of the conservation programs. Farmers suffer terrible damage from these animals. Tigers and leopards eat livestock and, occasionally, humans. Rhinoceros can ruin a farmer's entire crop in just one night. A troop of monkeys will eat through a field in an hour. It comes as no surprise then that most Nepalese feel they are competing with the same animals others are trying to save.

INTERNET LINKS

www.rbg-web2.rbge.org.uk/nepal/

Official website of the Royal Botanic Garden Edinburgh, with a webpage dedicated to Nepal and its plants, including many links and color images.

www.census.gov.np/

Official website of the national population census of Nepal.

www.crocodilenepal.org/

Website with detailed information on Nepalese crocodiles and the importance of their conservation.

HISTORY

The Durbar Square with the Royal Palace in Patan. The splendor of Nepal's architecture reflects a history of rich and advanced cultural traditions.

2

NEPAL'S EARLY HISTORY began in the Kathmandu Valley, which was once a lake. Geologists believe that the lake drained about 200,000 years ago, but the cause is unclear. Legend says that the god Manjushri sliced the valley wall at Chohar, where there is a narrow gorge, and drained the water.

The Hindu god Indra is said to have visited the valley of Kathmandu in the seventh or eighth century B.C. disguised as a human. There, Indra met with the king. Siddhartha Gautama, the founder of Buddhism, was

Previously an ancient Newar town and capital during the Malla Kingdom, Bhaktapur is now a UNESCO World Heritage Site for its rich culture, temples, and wood, metal, and stone artwork.

Nepal's recorded history is centered in the area around Kathmandu where the Kirantis are said to have ruled for many centuries beginning in the seventh century B.C. The Gopalas who were herdsmen are said to have ruled before the Kirantis. Very little is known about them even though their descendants are said to still live in the Kathmandu Valley.

A portrait of King Prithvi Narayan Shah, known as the "Father of the Nation." His military conquests united the warring states of Nepal.

born about 563 B.C. in Lumbini, a town located on the plains of Nepal's Terai. He is also believed to have visited Kathmandu during his travels.

Although much of the country's history is shrouded in myth, it is certain that by the time of the Licchavi Dynasty, Nepal's first golden age around A.D. 300, the religions of Hinduism and Buddhism had been firmly established. During those years, visitors from Chinese kingdoms marveled at the richness of the king's palace and courtyards. When the last Licchavi king died in A.D. 733, Nepal plunged into its dark age.

THE MALLAS

In 1200, the Malla Dynasty was established. Although the early Malla kings were strict Hindus, they established a tradition of peaceful coexistence with the Buddhists; this tradition is still strong today. The Malla kings were also able administrators who codified the Hindu caste system.

During the first three centuries of Malla rule, the valley endured many invasions from western Nepal and Muslims from northern India. As many as 80 small kingdoms in what is now Nepal fought each other to increase the size of their kingdoms. Muslims from Bengal did actually take over the valley in 1364. The Mallas regained control within a week, however, and the short Muslim occupation of the kingdom had no lasting influence.

The Mallas in the Kathmandu Valley prospered, and Nepal's second golden age began in the 15th century. The valley's three main cities—Kathmandu, Bhaktapur, and Patan—grew wealthy on the trade between India and Tibet. Most of the sculptures, woodcarvings, and buildings the valley is famous for today were built during this time.

Yaksha Malla (1428—82) was the greatest of the Malla kings. He ruled a kingdom far bigger than present-day Nepal. His kingdom was divided among his three sons. Their quarrels split the small Kathmandu Valley into three kingdoms—Kathmandu, Patan, and Bhaktapur. For the next 200 years, each

One of the most significant legacies of Nepal was its introduction of Buddhism to Tibet.

A Nepalese princess, Bhirkuti, was given in marriage to the powerful Tibetan king Songtsen Gampo. The king was the strongest, fiercest warrior of his day. He and his army were so feared that even the powerful Chinese sent a princess in marriage as a sign of respect. Bhirkuti's faith, however, was strong enough to convert the king and Tibet to Buddhism.

Bhirkuti is still loved in Tibet and worshiped as the Green Tara, a symbol of mercy and compassion. She is also worshiped by the Buddhists of Nepal.

kingdom built fine palaces, but their rulers—all cousins—schemed against one another, eventually causing their own downfall.

THE HOUSE OF SHAH

Sixty miles (96.5 km) west of Kathmandu, Prithvi Narayan Shah, king of the small Rajput kingdom of Gorkha, watched the bickering of Kathmandu's kings and decided to strike. He was a brave man, a good leader and strategist, and a good politician. He was also persistent: it took him more than 20 years to take Kathmandu. To his good fortune, even after he attacked the valley, the Malla kings refused to join as one army and fight back. Through battles and political intrigue, Prithvi Narayan Shah conquered the kingdoms one by one. In 1768 he finally managed to consolidate them and found the modern state of Nepal. He established the capital of Nepal at Kathmandu.

Jang Bahadur and his second wife. In 1850, Jang Bahadur Rana became the first Nepalese leader to travel to Britain and France. His family ruled Nepal for over a century.

Prithvi Narayan Shah and his successors expanded the kingdom until it included Sikkim in the east and a small area of Kashmir in the west. By the early 1800s, Nepal was one of the greatest powers in South Asia.

THE BRITISH

Nepal's expansion brought it into contact with the other expanding power of the time—Great Britain. In 1814 Nepal and Great Britain went to war over a territorial dispute. After some initial success on the Nepalese side, the British triumphed. The British forced Nepal to sign a treaty in 1816. This treaty reduced the country almost to its present size and gave Great Britain the right to station a representative in Kathmandu.

Irritated by the treaty they were forced to sign, the Nepalese gave the British representative the worst land in the valley, which was infested with malaria and "evil spirits." They also denied him the right to leave the valley except to go to and from India by a single route.

The experience left Nepal so resentful of foreigners that it closed its borders until 1951.

THE KOT MASSACRE

Nepal's defeat by the British threw the government into turmoil. Because of the treaty, ambitious members of the aristocracy had no opportunity to expand Nepal further. So they turned against each other instead and formed factions in a political war for control of Nepal.

In 1846 the queen's lover, Gagan Singh, was murdered during a palace intrigue. The furious queen gathered the various squabbling factions together in her *kot* (koht), meaning "fort," and accusations and insults flew. Hands reached for swords, and by the next morning, several dominant families had been wiped out. Jang Bahadur (1817—77), one of the faction leaders, survived.

Jang Bahadur appointed himself prime minister and was given the hereditary title of Rana. He and his family ruled Nepal for the next 115 years. The king was reduced to a mere puppet on the throne. The Ranas did nothing to improve the country and the lives of the people. When the Ranas were overthrown in 1951, only 5 percent of Nepal's population knew how to read and write.

THE RESTORATION OF MONARCHY

After India gained independence in 1947, pressure grew in Nepal for the Ranas to reform the government. There were even protests and strikes at factories in the Terai. The opposition was led by the able and charismatic B.P. Koirala, who operated from a base in India. In 1950, the king seized the initiative to depose the Ranas and restore the authority of the royal family. He first requested asylum in the Indian Embassy in Kathmandu.

King Tribhuvan was flown to India, where he demanded that the Ranas return power to him and the people of Nepal. The Ranas responded by declaring his crown null and void and appointing Tribhuvan's infant grandson king. All international governments refused to recognize the new infant king and expressed their support for King Tribhuvan.

King Tribhuvan Bir Bikram Shah was King of Nepal from 1911 until his death (not considering his exile from 1950 to 1951).

DEMOCRACY IN NEPAL

Tribhuvan declared his support for a democratic government. With popular support, the king took control of Nepal within a year. King Tribhuvan laid the foundation for parliamentary democracy before his death in 1955. In 1959 a constitution was adopted, and the first democratic election was held. The

New Nepal In My Vision

"Exercising People's democracy in 21st century, free from exploition, suppession and discrimination pertained to class, nation, region and sex, advancing in the form of a base area of the world revolution, becoming an ocean of armed people in order to prevent from counter- revolution, consolidated into one as in plain region of south including at the bottom of Himalayas by east-west highway and link roads in the midways, highly advanced by means of complete electrification and self- sustained economy, culturally prosperous in the form of a colourful garden with the provision of free education and health, a Nepalese society agitating for the sake of truth, goodness and beauty - herein lies my vision of a new Nepal."

Chairman : Com. Prachanda   Communist Party of Nepal (Maoist) District Organization Committe, Solukumbu

A slogan from the Maoist rebels. Many people were internally displaced as a result of the conflict, which disrupted the majority of rural development activities and led to a deep and complex transformation of Nepali society.

Nepali Congress Party led by B.P. Koirala gained power. But in 1960, after constant friction between the king and the Cabinet, Tribhuvan's son, King Mahendra, staged a coup and dissolved parliament. In 1962 a new constitution was adopted. All political parties were banned and the king was granted absolute power.

In 1979 discontent at rampant government corruption led to riots by the people. The king held a national referendum to decide whether to have a multiparty system or continue with the 1962 constitution. The king won by a narrow majority. Yet poverty and corruption persisted.

In 1990 after a series of bloody riots between leftist demonstrators and the police, in which hundreds of citizens were killed, King Birendra gave up most of his power to a democratically elected, multiparty parliament.

MAOIST REBELS

A Maoist guerrilla movement began in Nepal's countryside in 1996. The movement aimed to overthrow the government and set up a communist government in Nepal based on the ideals of China's Communist Revolution. The Maoist guerrillas spread throughout the nation and gained strength in the late 1990s. The Maoist rebels attacked government property, killing 14,000 civilians in the process. The rebels also had armed confrontations with Nepal's police. In July 2001, the Maoist rebels agreed to a ceasefire proposed by the government. In November 2001, talks between the rebels and the government failed, leading to a relaunch of attacks by the rebels. Nepal's decade-long civil war finally ended in November 2006 with a public holiday to celebrate. A peace deal was agreed between Maoist guerrillas and an alliance of seven political parties.

ROYAL TRAGEDY

In June 2001, King Birendra, Queen Aishwarya, their son Prince Nirajan, their daughter Princess Shruti, two of the king's sisters, his brother-in-law, and a cousin were all killed during a bloody shooting at the Narayanhiti royal palace. The official account maintains that Crown Prince Dipendra, King Birendra's son, shot most of the royal family before fatally wounding himself, after an argument with his parents over his choice of bride. Prince Gyanendra, King Birendra's brother, was crowned king three days after the shootings. King Gyanendra assumed the throne in exceptional circumstances in 2001. His reign was brief and unsettled. In December 2006 seven political parties agreed to abolish the monarchy. The country was declared a republic by the Maoist-led constituent assembly in May 2007.

The late Nepalese royal family. In the foreground sits King Birendra and Queen Aishwarya, while Princess Shruti, Crown Prince Dipendra and Prince Nirajan stand in the background.

INTERNET LINKS

www.ayo-gorkhali.org/

Website with information on the history and legacy of the British Gurkhas and their enduring ties with the people of the UK.

www.hindu.com/2001/07/29/stories/13290171.htm

The online edition of India's national newspaper contains links to many articles including one entitled Permanent rebellion: The story of B.P. Koirala.

www.the-voyagers.tripod.com/royaltragedy.htm

This website contains a link to an article titled Nepal's Royal Family. It tells of the circumstances surrounding the murder of King Birendra and most of his immediate family.

GOVERNMENT

Nepalese policemen gather outside the Singha Durbar government complex as Unified Communist Party of Nepal (Maoist) supporters protest in Kathmandu.

3

AFTER A BRIEF MOMENT of democracy—from 1959 to 1960—the monarchy reasserted control.

In 1990, after forceful "people power" demonstrations by mostly leftist protesters, King Birendra gave up his almost absolute power in favor of a parliamentary democracy.

The Nepali Congress Party won the 1991 parliamentary elections. Since then it has alternated in power with the Nepal Communist Party. A lack of stability and the general corruption of all Nepalese political parties, however, have led to widespread dissatisfaction among the people. In 2005 King Gyanendra appointed a series of prime ministers prior to sacking the entire government. He assumed complete control but antimonarchist demonstrations by hundreds of thousands of people heralded the end of direct palace rule in 2006. The newly formed Maoist-led government nationalized all royal properties including the palace but allowed the former king to live in Nepal as a tax-paying citizen. Civil unrest and political instability continued. In 2012 some politicians called for the resurrection of the monarchy.

ADMINISTRATIVE ORGANIZATION

Nepal is a federal democratic republic with 14 administrative divisions or *anchal* (AHN-chel). The legislative branch is a unicameral Constituent Assembly with 601 seats; 240 members are elected by direct popular vote, 335 are elected by proportional representation, and 26 are appointed by the Cabinet (Council of Ministers).

Since the king was overthrown there has been an interim constitution in place. In 2008 a Constituent Assembly was elected as an interim parliament with a mandate to draft and promote a new constitution by 2010. The deadline was extended four times, most recently until 2012.

"Nepal is like a yam between two boulders (China and India)."
—Prithvi Narayan Shah

The Constituent Assembly failed to draft a new constitution by the May 27 deadline which forced a November election of a new Assembly.

In 2011 the Cabinet was formed by a majority coalition made up of the United Communist Party of Nepal-Maoist, Madhesi People's Rights Forum-Nepal, Madhesi People's Rights Forum-Republic, Terai-Madhes Democratic Party, Madhesi People's Rights Forum-Democratic, and a number of smaller parties.

The president is elected by the parliament. In 2008 Ram Baran Yadav was elected president by the Constituent Assembly. In August 2011 Prime Minister Baburam Bhattarai came to power, with Deputy Prime Ministers Bijay Kumar Gachchadar and Narayan Kaji Shrestha.

Nepal is divided into 14 *anchal*, or zones. Each *anchal* is divided into *jilla* (JILL-lah), or districts. There are 75 *jillas*, each with a legislative assembly. Each district is divided into villages. Each village has a village assembly. Every Nepalese citizen aged 18 or above can vote in elections for village, district, and national assemblies.

PEOPLE POWER

Except for B.P. Koirala, who was democratically elected prime minister in 1959, Nepal has always been governed by a strong figure who came to power either by birthright or force, or both. The king was the government. Everyone was ultimately answerable to the king; the king answered only to himself.

Momentum for change came in the 1980s with the rise of a young, educated class. Economic growth was poor, opportunities for the educated were limited, and the foreign aid pouring into the country had little effect on their lives. Knowledge of international affairs meant the Nepalese were aware of "people power" movements in the Philippines and Eastern Europe. These events inspired them to demand change in Nepal.

Demonstrations broke out in 1990. On April 3 the army fired into a crowd of demonstrators near the royal palace killing 45 people. This tragic event led King Birendra to start the change to democracy. In 1991 the Nepali Congress Party won the first free election. The party's leader, G.P. Koirala—B.P. Koirala's brother—became prime minister. Since then, power has alternated between the Nepali Congress Party, a coalition of Communist parties, and the right-wing Rastriya Prajanatantra Party. Political bickering and power grabs, however, have prevented stability or progress in the nation.

NO STABILITY IN SIGHT

The Nepalese have grown disillusioned with democracy as political promises have turned out empty. In 1996 a Maoist rebellion developed in western Nepal, based on the beliefs of China's Mao Zedong. This Maoist movement spread to the whole country and became increasingly violent. Thousands have died, many of them members of Nepal's police force. In 2001 the government entered into the first face-to-face talks with the Maoists, but a settlement was not reached until 2006.

Nepal's political situation was further aggravated on June 1, 2001, after the killing of almost the entire royal family. Birendra's only surviving brother, Gyanendra, was crowned king amid much public outrage, as many Nepalese doubted the official explanation of the killings, which pointed to Crown Prince Dipendra as the sole culprit.

Nepal's politicians have not been able to agree a constitution since the decade-old Maoist insurgency ended in 2006. Without a new constitution there is a risk of protracted political instability and violence. A Constituent Assembly election will be held in November 2013 after being continually delayed for years by the election comission of Nepal. The parties running are the Unified Communist Party of Nepal (Maoist), the Nepali Congress and the Communist Party of Nepal (UML), among others.

INTERNET LINKS

www.nepalgov.gov.np/
Official website of the government of Nepal.

www.gpkcenter.org/index.php/gp-koirala.html
Official website of the GPK Foundation, including a political profile of G.P. Koirala.

www.ucpnm.org/english/index.php
Official website of the Unified Communist Party of Nepal (Maoist).

ECONOMY

Rice fields seen below the Lukla Everest region of Nepal. Rice is the staple food throughout the country.

4

BY ANY MEASURE, Nepal is one of the poorest and most underdeveloped countries in the world. The per capita income is only about $1,300 a year. This figure ranks Nepal as one of the 20 poorest countries in the world.

Nepal's harsh geography, the lack of almost any natural resources, the severe lack of skilled labor, and political instability make improving the economic situation very difficult.

There is a huge income distribution gap. The lowest 10 percent of households receive only 3.2 percent of the national income. The top 10 percent receives 29.5 percent. Around 25 percent of the population lives below the poverty line.

Women in the eastern Terai bundling harvested rice on the fields.

Nepal had an isolated and agrarian society until the middle of the 20th century with poor infrastructure, few schools and hospitals, and very little industry. The country has made progress toward sustainable economic growth, but political uncertainty and civil unrest have hampered the development toward economic progress.

Cobs of yellow corn drying near Ulleri, along the Annapurna trail.

More than 65 percent of the labor force relies on agriculture. Large areas of the Middle Hills suffer from a food deficit, which means that farmers cannot produce enough to feed their families. The government must rely on food aid and imports to feed the population. Many farmers in the Middle Hills are forced to seek seasonal work in the lowlands and in India.

Agriculture accounts for 38 percent of the gross domestic product (GDP). Industry, mainly carpets and textiles, accounts for 15 percent. The service sector, mainly tourism, contributes 47 percent.

Economists estimate Nepal needs an annual growth rate of 6 percent to achieve any real economic progress. In the early 1990s, Nepal actually achieved this growth figure, which has since dropped to 4.6 percent.

AGRICULTURE

In Nepal agriculture depends on altitude, because changes in altitude affect the climate. Rice, for example, can only be grown up to about 6,500 feet (1,981 m). Corn, wheat, and millet can be grown higher, up to about 9,000 feet (2,743 m). In the highest altitudes, up to about 14,000 feet (4,267 m), people depend on corn, buckwheat, and potatoes.

Agriculture depends on water, too. Irrigation is usually necessary to grow rice. The higher the altitude, the fewer the sources of water, thus growing rice becomes more difficult. Below 2,100 feet (640 m), in the Terai, on the other hand, it is often possible to grow two crops of rice a year.

Rice and wheat are the main crops in the Terai region, while corn is the main crop in the hills and mountain areas. Apart from rice, wheat, and corn, Nepal's principal crops are millet, buckwheat, barley, potatoes, sugarcane, lentils, and jute. Cabbages, cauliflower, beans, okra, and tomatoes are major vegetables. The fertile Terai produces a sizable surplus, but production is influenced by climatic conditions, low agricultural productivity, and lack of modern technology, and so it is still not enough to feed the entire population. In addition, it is better for Nepal's economy to accept food aid and sell the surplus.

INDUSTRY

The industrial sector in Nepal is very undeveloped. In 1960 there were only 63 registered industries which were struggling to survive because of poor organization and infrastructure. Until the mid-1980s, Nepal's leading export was jute, a fiber spun from the jute plant and used to weave burlap bags. In the late 1980s Nepal's carpet industry gave Nepal its first industrial boom.

The carpet industry has its roots in the Tibetan refugee community. Swiss relief workers working with Tibetan refugees discovered three individuals who knew traditional designs and carpet-making techniques and worked with them to develop a carpet industry as a way for the refugees to earn money.

The carpets became popular in Europe, particularly in Germany. Soon, the Tibetans were not the only ones making carpets; factories using Nepalese workers sprang up all over the Kathmandu Valley.

Tibetan women weaving carpets at a refugee settlement. Carpet weaving is an important sector in the export economy of Nepal.

The boom subsided when consumers discovered that carpet production required a great deal of child labor and caused pollution. The industry tried to clean up its labor and environmental practices, but problems still remain and the carpet industry has been badly affected.

In the late 1990s, pashmina shawls woven in Nepal became popular around the world. Pashmina is the cashmere-like hair of mountain goats. Export of pashminas nearly doubled from the year 2000 to 2001.

A mix of modern and cottage industries is slowly developing thanks to foreign aid targeted at both communications and transportation infrastructure. In recent years Nepal has started to export metal statues, filigree goods and utensils, hand carved wooden objects, and other handicraft goods.

TOURISM

Nepal's largest service industry by far is tourism. The country is a tourist's dream, blessed with stunning natural beauty and beautiful monuments. Major attractions for tourists include mountain climbing, trekking, bird watching, rock climbing, river rafting, and jungle safaris. The royal tragedy combined with political instability since 1990 have had a negative impact on tourism. In 2010 more than 600,000 tourists visited Nepal. Of these, more than 100,000 came from India, 45,000 from Sri Lanka, 43,000 from China, and 37,000 from the United States.

Unfortunately, an estimated 60 percent of the foreign currency earned from tourism leaves Nepal. It pays for imported goods to support tourism; little money actually goes into the pockets of the people.

Trekking, a popular tourist activity, makes heavy demands on Nepal's ecosystem. For instance, firewood needed to cook meals and heat hot water for trekkers is obtained by cutting down trees. Locals have opposed calls for Mount Everest to be restricted due to environmental damage, because many of them rely on tourism for income. For example, sherpas (mountain guides) can make about $2,000 or more per expedition.

There is also a movement for more responsible tourism. Launched in 1986, the Annapurna Conservation Area Project (ACAP) collects fees from visitors and works with local communities in developmental programs. Its stated goal is to achieve sustained balance between nature conservation and socio-economic improvement in the Annapurna Conservation Area.

TRADE

About 59 percent of Nepal's trade is with India. The trade balance is skewed heavily in India's favor. The situation is the same with its other trading partners—the amount of goods Nepal imports from these countries is three times more than the amount of goods it is able to export to them.

DEVELOPMENT AID

Some cynical critics maintain that foreign aid, not tourism, is Nepal's leading industry. In 1998, 70 percent of Nepal's development budget came from foreign sources. Development aid, in the form of grants and loans, accounted for 10 percent of the GDP that year.

Aid from foreign governments often funds projects to build road networks, water and electrical systems, and other infrastructure. Much of the aid given to Nepal goes out of the country to pay foreign contractors hired to carry out the projects. Japan, India, the United States, and many European countries are the major donors to Nepal.

International bodies, such as the UN, the World Bank, and the Asian Development Bank, also fund big projects in Nepal. These projects often are criticized for ignoring the concerns of the local people. Foreign aid is extremely important to Nepal and is considered essential to support the peace process and the country's recovery form 10 years of civil unrest. Nepal received $1.1 billion of official development assistance (ODA) in the fiscal year 2010 to 2011. ODA financed more than 40 percent of capital expenditure and 21 percent of all government expenditure in that year.

Nongovernmental organizations (NGOs), such as CARE, Save the Children, and Oxfam International, are also active in Nepal. Their projects are often carried out on a smaller scale and involve mostly social development work.

A young boy in Potters Square in Bhaktapur molding clay on a pottery wheel made from a used truck tire. Many development projects are aimed at improving Nepal's social conditions, especially for that of the children.

INTERNET LINKS

www.doanepal.gov.np/index.php

Official website of the Department of Agriculture, with information and statistics on agriculture in Nepal.

www.tourism.gov.np/

Official website of the Ministry of Culture, Tourism and Civil Aviation, with links to major tourism activities, sites, and associations.

www.ntnc.org.np/home

Official website of the National Trust for Nature Conservation in Nepal, with links to information on ACAP and other NTNC projects.

ENVIRONMENT

Wild cows roaming along the Himalayan mountain meadows.

5

THE SOARING HIMALAYAN mountains seem to embody strength and power, but like the rest of Nepal's landscape, the Himalaya is extremely fragile and vulnerable to deforestation. Nepal relies heavily on traditional energy resources as no significant deposits of fossil fuels have been found.

The Nepalese rely on trees for most of their energy needs. Most people cook and heat using only firewood. Trees provide 75 percent of the country's total energy consumption, petroleum 9 percent, electricity only 2 percent, and hydropower less than 1 percent despite the immense potential. Approximately 40 percent of the population has access to electricity. Of this, 33 percent comes from the National grid and 7 percent from alternative energy. As Nepal's population is rapidly increasing, more trees need to be cut to meet the rising energy needs. Hillsides devoid of trees erode rapidly and, in the process, lose their productive soil. Without this rich soil, fields become barren and vital crops will not thrive.

The rising number of people migrating to the Kathmandu Valley from the countryside has resulted in an increased number of motor vehicles in the capital city. Air pollution levels in Nepal are now among the highest in the world.

Nepal's rich and diverse wildlife is also increasingly being threatened. Recent conservation efforts to save the Bengal tiger, the Asian one-horned rhinoceros, the gharial crocodile, the Ganges freshwater dolphin, and the snow leopard have met with some success, but most of these

The natural environment in Nepal has suffered from deforestation and soil erosion, agricultural encroachment, and contamination of the water supply. The primary cause of decline in forestland is the cutting of trees for use as firewood. A number of government initiatives have been introduced to address these environmental issues.

species continue to be threatened with extinction. In addition, plants that have been used as herbal remedies for centuries are taken from the hills to meet the strong demand for them in other countries. Most of these plants are smuggled to India.

Hundreds of streams and rivers flowing down Nepal's mountains and hills give the country the potential to generate 83 million MW of electricity, enough power to supply the whole of Great Britain. However, Nepal's hostile geography, coupled with the country's scarce economic resources, makes this great potential difficult to develop.

DEFORESTATION

In the 1950s the government nationalized and centralized the management of all of Nepal's forests. Prior to this, each village had managed its own forest area. The villagers made sure to conserve and nurture the land that provided them with their only source of food. Once the forests were nationalized, developers exploited the forests for financial profit.

Rich forests full of valuable trees once covered Nepal's Terai. Migration to the Terai has resulted in forests being cleared. Tree roots absorb runoff from the monsoon rains, keeping the fields from flooding. Trees also slow down the flow of rainwater by blocking the path of runoff. As the fields become barren, runoff increases, washing away the productive topsoil from fields. These floods also kill livestock and dozens of people annually.

WILDLIFE CONSERVATION

Nepal's abundant and exotic wildlife is worth preserving not only because of its importance to the environment but also because of its great economic potential—every year thousands of tourists come to Nepal to see the country's amazing wildlife.

Japanese tourists mount the elephant that will take them on a safari at the Island Jungle Resort hotel in the Royal Chitwan National Park.

FIREWOOD ALTERNATIVES

Starting in the late 1980s and throughout the 1990s, Nepal's government reversed its former policy by giving control of the forests back to the local people. Foreign aid donors sponsored projects to create tree nurseries. A forest conservation program includes village tree nurseries and free distribution of seedlings. Wood burning stoves were provided to increase energy efficiency and reduce the amount of wood needed for fuel. "Community forests" are now a part of most villages again.

Deforestation, nevertheless, remains a serious problem, as most Nepalese still depend on trees for firewood, fodder for livestock, and building materials. As Nepal's population continues to increase at a rate of 1.8 percent a year, forest resources will continue to decrease.

The ACAP alternative energy (AE) program aims to reduce the use of forest resources and provide energy alternatives to firewood. Villagers are encouraged to use fuel efficient heating and cooking devices and alternative energy, such as back boilers, smoke water heaters, solar heaters, kerosene stoves, and improved stoves. Local kerosene depots have been established in the villages.

The AE program in the Manaslu Conservation Area Project (MCAP) includes the installation of kerosene depots. Four micro-hydro power stations are in operation. These measures aim to reduce pressure on regional forests. Where micro-hydro power is not possible the villagers have been provided with solar lighting facilities. Local operators are also available to provide training in the implementation of these systems.

The Biodiversity Conservation Center (BCC) is also part of the National Trust for Nature Conservation (NTNC). It also aims to reduce the pressure on the forests due to extraction of fuel wood. To achieve this goal alternative energy devices, such as biogas, husk stoves, and improved cooking stoves, are distributed to the communities living on the fringe of Chitwan National Park.

Alternative energy devices such as biogas plants have also been installed as part of the Bardia Conservation Program (BCP) and the Suklaphanta Conservation Program (SCP).

The Nepali government established wildlife preserves long before their benefits were recognized and often in the face of local opposition. Nepal's most famous national park, Chitwan National Park, grew out of a royal hunting preserve.

Although many animals continue to face extinction, valuable breeding projects have at least stabilized endangered populations. There are now about 200 Bengal tigers and 500 greater one-horned rhinoceros, a sixth of their worldwide population, in Chitwan National Park.

Chitwan National Park has grown into Nepal's second most popular tourist destination (second only to Kathmandu) thanks to the cooperation of the local people. At first, there were only a few exclusive hotels near the park that catered to wealthy tourists. Revenue from these hotels had little effect on the lives of the local people, as most of the money earned was used to pay for the imported goods needed by the tourists.

At night, wildlife from the park used to cross the river surrounding the preserve and destroy farmers' crops. As the number of tourists on a low budget increased, inexpensive hotels owned and run by Nepalese sprung up around the edges of the park. Since these hotels employed the local people, the community's economy improved. There was also more money generated to pay for the upkeep of the park; thus, fences were built around the park to keep the animals inside.

In 1995 the government of Nepal entrusted the management of Nepal's Central Zoo in the Kathmandu Valley to NTNC for 30 years. Central Zoo was a private zoo established in 1932 by the late Rana Prime Minister Juddha Shamsher. After the political changes of 1950 it remained under the management of various government departments before it was handed over to NTNC on the occasion of the Golden Jubilee Birthday Celebration of the Late Majesty King Birendra in December 1995. The trust aims to develop the zoo as a center for wildlife research and conservation and to generate public awareness and participation in wildlife and nature conservation.

INCENTIVES FOR NATIONAL PARKS Some local and international incentives have given Chitwan and the local community a boost. In 1993 the Fourth Amendment to the National Parks and Wildlife Conservation Act was passed to establish a buffer zone and set aside half the park fees for local use, which includes relocation of communities living within the park's boundaries. The NTNC has worked with villagers to set up tours of local community forests. The United Nations Development Program also works with local communities. The long-term objective is to involve the local people in nature and wildlife conservation. There are proposals to further develop the buffer zone around the park and link it with animal migration routes to parks in India.

AIR POLLUTION

In the 1980s large numbers of Nepalese from the countryside migrated to the Kathmandu Valley to work in the carpet and garment industries. The amount of traffic in the valley grew with the population. Vehicular emissions cause particulate air pollution and are the prime source of air pollution in Kathmandu.

A Nepali man reading a newspaper while wearing a mask to help filter the terrible air pollution in Kathmandu.

A UN report issued in 2002 stated that the air quality in Kathmandu was probably the worst in the world. The valley's bowl-like shape holds in exhaust pollutants. In 2012 the Environment Performance Index (EPI) ranked Nepal among the three worst countries in the world in terms of air quality and the effects on human health. Worldwide studies have concluded that there is a significant association between particulate matter air pollutants and health effects such as lung cancer, respiratory and cardiovascular disease, and mortality.

Tiny three-wheeled vehicles called *tempo* (TEM-po) are the worst polluters. To cut down pollution levels people are encouraged to use electric *tempos* that have been introduced as private and public transport vehicles. There are currently 650 *tempos* operating in the city. These vehicles also provide employment for more than 1,000 Nepalese everyday. Three-wheeled electric vehicles are replacing smoke-belching diesel vehicles. Based on the success of the three-wheeled electric *tempos* a safer and more modern electric bus has also been developed and introduced. Planting trees and shrubs in the city to improve air quality is also encouraged.

Minerals and bacteria color a lake below Jharkot along the Annapurna circuit.

WATER PROBLEMS

The carpet boom of the 1980s certainly helped the Nepali economy, but the environmental damage was also great. There were few environmental regulations in place at the time and they were not enforced. Carpet factories simply dumped waste directly into the valley's rivers or into pits dug at the factories. As a consequence, Kathmandu's rivers are polluted.

Fifty percent of the water in Kathmandu's water system is of "unsatisfactory" quality according to international standards. Poor quality pipes are partly to blame. In some estimates, 50 percent of the water leaks out from the pipes as pollutants and sewage leak in. People must boil and filter their water. In the dry season, long lines of people wait for hours near public taps for only a few minutes of water flow a day. Over-extraction of groundwater has left the reservoirs on the verge of drying out, leaving 75 percent of the city without a regular water supply.

The Himalayan Light Foundation (HLF) has introduced SPOWTS to provide completely pathogen-free clean drinking water for villagers and tourists. By combining the use of solar photovoltaic (solar PV) systems with the income generating activity of selling clean water the sustainability of the system is assured and also provides an income for the system owners. The system also reduces the number of plastic water bottles, which helps to minimize pollution.

MELTING GLACIERS

Nepal has not escaped the consequences of global warming. According to a report by the Worldwatch Institute, the ice in the Himalayan glaciers is expected to shrink by 20 percent by the year 2035.

A lake of melted ice now sits behind a natural dam at Imja Glacier in the Everest region. In the 1950s a very thick layer of ice covered the Imja glacier. Meltwater ponds developed and merged and by the 1970s had formed the Imja lake. By 2007 the Imja lake was about 0.68 miles (1.1 km) long with an average depth of 137.8 feet (42 m). The water is expected to burst out of the natural catchment area sometime in the future and cascade in to the valley below. In 1985 a similar glacial lake burst, hurtling water for 56 miles (90 km) downstream, washing away fields, homes, livestock, and people.

The beautiful glacial Imja lake, along the Solu Khumbu Everest Region in Sagarmatha National Park.

INTERNET LINKS

www.wwfnepal.org/

Official website of the World Wildlife Fund in Nepal. This site has many links to WWF news and information articles relevant to Nepal.

www.forestrynepal.org/

Website with information on forestry in Nepal.

www.hlf.org.np/

Official website of the HLF, a nongovernmental organization (NGO) working in Nepal. HLF's main objective is to introduce and use environment-friendly renewable energy technologies.

www.itnsource.com/shotlist//ITN/2009/12/01/T01120908/

Website with link to an informative video about the Imja glacier meltwater lake.

NEPALESE

A Tibetan family dressed in their traditional outfits during *Losar*, a Tibetan and Sherpa New Year festival, at the Bodhnath Buddhist stupa.

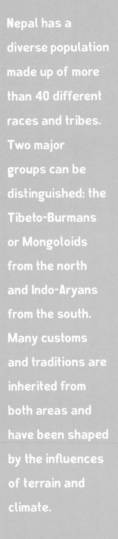

6

T HERE ARE DOZENS OF DISTINCT ethnic groups in Nepal. Although these groups have been living together for hundreds of years, there has been little blending or mixing. But there has always been a great deal of tolerance among the groups.

In Nepal, neighbors may worship different gods and speak different languages, but nobody thinks there is anything strange about that. Nepalese like to compare the different ways of their lives, and the unique customs of the various ethnic groups are a favorite topic of conversation among the local people.

Nepal has a diverse population made up of more than 40 different races and tribes. Two major groups can be distinguished: the Tibeto-Burmans or Mongoloids from the north and Indo-Aryans from the south. Many customs and traditions are inherited from both areas and have been shaped by the influences of terrain and climate.

Women and children in their dolpo blankets gather at a Tibetan Buddhist festival in the Do Tarap Valley in Dolpo.

High caste Brahmin boys learning religious Hindu formulas called "mantra" at a school (*gurukul*) in Janakpur.

Nepal is a very hierarchical society, influenced by the caste system that originated in the dominant religion, Hinduism, and was codified by the early Malla kings. The hill groups are outside the caste system, but they have a class system of their own. Each group is divided into clans. These clans, in turn, are further subdivided into extended families. Nepal's population can be divided into four main groups: the Hindu caste groups, the hill tribes, the Bhote, and the Newar.

HINDU CASTE GROUPS

The people of the Hindu caste groups migrated to Nepal between the 12th and 15th centuries, when they were driven from their homes in India by Muslim invaders. They were originally of Aryan stock and have Caucasian features, but with a darker complexion. They brought with them their Indo-Aryan language, which evolved into Nepali, Nepal's national language.

The Hindu religion has a strict hierarchy known as the caste system. There are four main groups within the caste system: Brahmins (BRAH-mins), Chhetris (CHE-trees), Vaisyas (VIE-siahs), and Sudras (SOO-drahs). Hindus believe that humans sprang from the body of Brahma, the god and creator of everything. Brahmins came from Brahma's head and mouth, Chhetris from his arms, Vaisyas from his thighs, and Sudras from his feet.

At the top of the Hindu caste system are the Brahmins, the priests and scholars. Most Brahmin castes are strictly vegetarian and they are forbidden by tradition to drink alcohol and eat certain foods such as onions and tomatoes. A Brahmin must officiate at religious events, and they are the only group allowed to read the Hindu religious texts.

Below the Brahmins are the Chhetris, the warriors. They are traditionally the military or ruling class. Many of Nepal's army officers were Chhetri, and even today many Chhetris join the military.

Only Brahmins and Chhetris have the right to wear the *janai* (jyah-NIGH), the sacred thread draped across the chest that symbolizes that the wearer is born twice, the first time by his mother and the second time when he is initiated into Hinduism. The three intertwined threads are the symbol of high status.

Below the Brahmins and the Chhetris are the Vaisyas, the caste of merchants and tradesmen. Below them, at the bottom of the caste system, are the Sudras, or the occupational caste.

OCCUPATIONAL CASTES

At the lower end of the Hindu hierarchy are the occupational castes. People of these castes take their names from the traditional jobs they perform. Some examples are: *Kami* (KAH-mee), or blacksmiths; *Damai* (dah-MY), or tailors and musicians; and *Sarki* (SERH-kee), or cobblers.

The Sudras are traditionally looked down by the rest of Nepalese society. Many of them have to endure discrimination all their lives, even from the casteless hill tribes. Some Nepalese will not allow people from the occupational castes inside their homes. People who follow any religion other than Hinduism are traditionally considered to be Sudras and are considered impure, polluted, and untouchable. With the development of tourism as a major industry in the rural villagers the local people have stopped treating tourists as untouchables.

A friendly tailor plys his trade at the at Durbar Square of Kathmandu. Although vital to the community, jobs like these are considered to be the lowest form of work, and people who do these jobs are looked down on. This attitude is, however, slowly changing.

Today, the caste system is slowly being abandoned. Many Sudras have abandoned their traditional occupations and work as porters or day laborers. Ready-made clothes, shoes, and tools have made most of their traditional occupations unnecessary. Today, some Sudra work in high-profile government jobs just as some Brahmins and Chhetri are adopting traditional low-caste work. Caste-based discrimination is becoming less common, particularly in the cities, but it still exists in some rural villages.

HILL PEOPLES

The ancestors of Nepal's many hill groups crossed the high mountain passes from Tibet or followed the mountain trails from Burma. The hill peoples have Mongoloid features and speak their own languages.

The hill groups cluster in villages at altitudes of 6,000 to 9,000 feet (1,829-2,743 m). The Gurung live in the shadow of the Annapurna mountain and are known for their strength, endurance, and bravery. Young men from these groups predominate in the famous Gurkha regiments of the British army. The word Gurkha is a geographical term that refers to the Gurung, who originally came from the fortress town of Goraknath. Although these groups are casteless, they are subdivided into clans of different status. The Gurung, for example, have four upper clans and 16 lower ones.

A Kirati shepherd in the Manaslu region with his traditional *khukuri* knife.

Hill peoples, notably the Tamang, practice a religion that is often a mix of Tibetan Buddhism combined with Hindu teachings and sometimes animism or shamanism. They are often less conservative than caste Hindus and are more open in their relationships. Teenage boys and girls will openly flirt and court each other, behavior that is almost never seen among their Hindu caste neighbors.

Most hill peoples work as farmers, but they also keep large herds of goats and sheep. They sell the wool and meat from their herds in the market. Every year some members of every family must take the family's sheep and goats to high pastures of 12,000 to 14,000 feet (3,658—4,267 m), where it is easy to obtain good fodder for their herds.

RAI AND LIMBU Also known as Kirati, these two ethnic groups live throughout the eastern hills of Nepal extending across the border into India. The men of these groups often carry a large *khukuri* (KHOO-koo-ree), the traditional Nepali knife with a curved blade, tucked into a long cloth wrapped around the waist.

The Kirati group is famous for beautiful stone masonry of their farm terraces. They also build *chautara* (CHOW-tah-rah), stone resting platforms topped by large, shady pipal trees, on the trail outside villages as memorials to the dead.

TAMANG Tamang are the largest of the hill groups. They are also the most independent, retaining their own language and Buddhist religion even as other groups fall under increasing Nepali and Hindu influence. In Tibetan, tamang means "horse trader."

Tamang live in the high hills in the north, east, and west of Kathmandu. Traditionally the Tamang are farmers but they often come to the city to work as porters and day laborers.

A Tamang man may marry any girl from any clan except his own or his brother's clan. The preferred marriage partner is one's cross-cousin. For a man, that is either his father's sister's daughter or his mother's brother's daughter. Parallel-cousin marriage of a man to his father's brother's daughter or mother's sister's daughter is not allowed. Children of one's father's brother belong to the same clan as oneself.

Girls wearing the traditional Tamang costume in Nepal.

GURUNG Gurung live in the hills around Pokhara and east toward Gorkha. They, and the Magar, formed the bulk of Prithvi Narayan Shah's army when he conquered the Kathmandu Valley.

The military is still the main profession of the Gurung. Most families have at least one member serving in India or in the British army. Retired soldiers and their pensions are funding growth in Pokhara and other traditional Gurung hill areas.

Those remaining at home turn to farming and goat rearing. From April to September, a member of the family will take the sheep, cows, and water buffalo to high pastures, some above 14,000 feet (4,267 m).

MAGAR Like the Gurung, the Magar also live in the hill regions of central and western Nepal. In the 17th century, they had a very strong kingdom in what is now Palpa, and Prithvi Narayan Shah also depended heavily on them for his armies. Even today, the Magar send the greatest number of men to the military.

The northernmost Magar are essentially Buddhists, while those living further south have been heavily influenced by Hinduism. Their language is Magar Kura, a Tibeto-Burmese tongue.

SHERPAS Saying "Sherpa" has become the equivalent of saying "mountain guide" to most tourists, but the term should only be used for a group living mainly in the high valleys of the Everest region. In the Tibetan language it means people of the east.

Born at an altitude of more than 12,000 feet (3,658 m), at the base of the highest mountains in the world, Sherpas are naturally acclimatized to high-altitude mountain climbing.

Sherpas settled in the Everest area about 300 years ago after crossing over from Tibet. They were well known as traders long before they earned their fame as mountain porters and guides.

REMOTE GROUPS

There are several ethnic groups in Nepal that do not fit into any of the major groups:

THARU are the indigenous people of the Terai. Their natural immunity to malaria allowed them to survive in the jungle for centuries before modern insecticides opened the Terai to other Nepalese.

Living as marginal farmers in settlements scattered throughout the thick jungle this is the largest and oldest ethnic group of the Terai. Farming and business are their main occupations and they follow the Hindu religion.

CHEPANG are a group of people living in the most remote areas of the southern-middle hills of central Nepal. Shy around outsiders, they lived until recently as hunter-gatherers, woodcutters, and sometimes farmers.

They were severely exploited by their better-educated, more aggressive caste Hindu neighbors. The government has started several programs to help them.

Little boys relaxing in their hammocks in a Tharu village in Chitwan National Park.

BHOTES

Across Nepal's north, in high valleys of more than 9,000 feet (2,743 m), are groups of people called Bhotiya or Bhotes. The Bhote culture is essentially Tibetan (Bho is another name for Tibet).

Isolated by the Himalayan mountains, they live as farmers, sheep and yak herders, and lately as hoteliers to the tourist trade. They are also known as traders, traveling far beyond Nepal's borders.

MUSLIMS

Small communities of Muslim traders arrived in Kathmandu from Kashmir in the 15th century and again in the 17th century during the reign of Pratap Mall (1641-74).

A responsible elder sister takes care of her sibling in Nupri. In the hills, where infant mortality is high, families often have many children.

After the Indian Mutiny of 1857—a revolt led by Indian soldiers against British rule—some Muslim refugees fleeing India settled in Nepal. The British eventually defeated the Indian soldiers after a bloody retaliation with some help from Nepalese forces. For its contribution in helping the British put down the mutiny, Nepal received land that had belonged to the Nawab of Oudh, one of the mutiny's leaders. This area, including Nepalganj in the west, is the center of Islamic culture in present-day Nepal.

Unlike in India, Nepal's Hindu and Islamic cultures have always coexisted peacefully.

NEWAR

The Newar are the indigenous inhabitants of the Kathmandu Valley, where they have been living for the past 2,000 years. Their language originated from a mixture of Tibeto-Burmese and Sanskrit. The Newari language is one of the most complex languages in the world.

There are Newar communities in many of Nepal's larger towns. Almost all Newar work as merchants and shopkeepers. It was the Newar who built most of the temples and crafted most of the sculptures for which Kathmandu is famous.

The Newar have a highly structured caste system that the Malla kings dictated more than 600 years ago. As the Kathmandu Valley modernizes, old caste restrictions on occupation are slowly fading. However, the social restrictions of the caste system are still largely observed. The Newar very rarely marry outside their caste, and those who do risk being cut off from their community by their family and friends.

INTERNET LINKS

www.factsanddetails.com/world.php?itemid=1340&catid=55&subcatid=354

Website with a section on world religions, including details on Hinduism and the caste system.

www.visitnepal.com/nepal_information/people.php

Website with detailed information on Nepal, including a section on Nepal's people and ethnic groups.

www.nepal-tourism.net/Nepal_People.htm

Website of tour operator specializing in Nepal, with information on the people, festivals, arts, and culture.

Newar women clad in their traditional attire at the Jyapu Day celebrations in Kathmandu. Thousands of ethnic Newar people celebrate Jyapu Day, especially in Kathmandu, marking the end of the harvest season.

LIFESTYLE

Women selling flower garlands, mostly in front of the popular temples, to be used as offerings in Hindu rituals.

7

THERE ARE SO MANY different cultures in Nepal that the way people think and do things can vary tremendously from one house to the next. Neighbors may speak a different language, worship different gods, even celebrate a different day as New Year's Day. To a Nepalese, this is natural and everyone is extremely tolerant of the different traditions people hold.

Each cultural group in Nepal has a hierarchical structure. There are divisions and rankings within a family, an extended family, an ethnic group, and society as a whole. This system is something to which the Nepalese have grown accustomed.

In the villages, many household chores, such as laundry, take place outside the home.

The Nepalese people are made up of nearly 70 different cultural and linguistic groups living in different regions of the country. Most of these groups follow their own religion, speak their own language or dialect, and have their own traditional costumes and foods. However, as a result of globalization and tourists visiting the country many Nepalese now speak English and wear Western-style clothes, especially in the city of Kathmandu.

The caste system has been outlawed by the government but still plays a large role in everyday life. Attitudes are slowly changing, particularly in urban areas, and low-caste people do not carry the stigma they once did. The government is trying to widen opportunities for everyone.

Names in Nepal say more about the person than would a Western name. Names indicate one's caste or group, one's profession, and even where one is from.

If one met Mr. Khatiwada, one would know from his name that he is a Brahmin and probably from western Nepal. Mr. Pokhrel is a Brahmin, too, but from the east. Mr. Shakya is a Newar and works as a silversmith or goldsmith. As there are many rules regarding interaction between castes, knowing people's names settles the question of whether one can accept the rice they cook or visit their home. These customs are no longer as widely practiced as they were before.

A smiling Gurung family in the yard of their traditional farm house in the Annapurna region of Nepal. Even among the poorest families, parents cherish and often indulge their children.

FAMILY STRUCTURE

When Nepalese say "my family," they are speaking of their extended family. Cousins are called "brothers and sisters," a mother's oldest sister is called "oldest mother," a father's youngest brother is "youngest father," and so on.

Several generations commonly live under the same roof. Sons customarily stay in the home after marriage, bringing their wife to live with them and raising their children in their family homes.

The money earned by every member of the family goes into a treasury that is controlled by the head of the household, usually the oldest male. He has the final say in all important family decisions, such as children's education, jobs, and marriage partners.

Bhote women have a stronger position at home than most other Nepalese woman. As Bhote men are away from home trading most of the time, the women make most of the household decisions.

GROWING UP

Name-giving is the first important milestone for an infant in a Hindu home. Customs vary from group to group, but the name is determined by an astrologer based on the exact time of birth.

A baby in Birgunj is given rice as part of *pausni*, a weaning ceremony in Nepal.

Almost all groups have a rice-feeding ceremony called *pausni* (PAHS-nee) when a baby is about six-months old. Many guests are invited for this ceremony, and the parents will hold a big feast. Guests often give the child money to wish them future prosperity.

During a Newar *pausni*, several objects may be placed in front of the baby—dirt, unhusked rice, a brick, toys, a pen, or a hook. The parents and priest predict the child's future talents or occupation based on which object the infant reaches for first.

At about the age of five, male Brahmins and Chhetris have their head shaved except for a small tuft of hair toward the back of the head called a *tupi* (TOO-pee). The *tupi* indicates that the boy is a Hindu.

PUBERTY

When approaching puberty, male Brahmins and Chhetris receive a *janai*, a sacred thread made up of three loops of cotton twine, worn over the right shoulder and under the left arm. The *janai* is a sign of high caste and is changed once a year, during the full moon of July or August. After completing this ceremony, the boy is allowed to eat with other adult men.

At the age of 12, Buddhist boys have their heads shaved, are bathed, dressed in saffron robes, given alms bowls, and sent off begging, as the Buddha did thousands of years ago. However, the boys are sent only to the homes of their relatives and neighbors and return home on the same day.

Before they reach puberty, Newar girls go through their first marriage—to a *bel* (bale), a wood apple. The *bel* represents the god Subarna Kumar. Since the full marriage rites can only be performed once, their subsequent marriage is of secondary importance and they are free to divorce and remarry.

In Hindu and Newar homes, a daughter reaching puberty is no cause for celebration. During their first menstruation, they are locked in a room for 14 days. Considered unclean, they are forbidden to see or be seen by the men of the house or to touch any food but their own. Sometimes even the women of their own house avoid their touch.

MARRIAGE

Almost all marriages in Nepal are between members of the same caste or ethnic group. Intercaste marriages are extremely rare, as both husband and wife will be cut off from their respective families.

Hindu and Newar marriages are usually arranged. A relative of either the bride or groom acts as a go-between, carrying photos of the boy and girl and persuading both sets of parents. Sometimes the couple is allowed to meet, but only if accompanied by many chaperones.

There are three types of marriages among the hill groups: arranged marriages, free courtship, or "kidnapping." Once the boy "kidnaps" the girl of his choice, he has three days to convince her to marry him. If she refuses, he must release her. Wedding customs vary widely from group to group.

Although it is illegal, polygamy, or having more than one spouse at any one time, still occurs in Nepal. As Islam allows it, Muslims are exempted from this law. The most common reason for taking another wife is the inability of the first wife to bear a son. All the wives may live together or separately.

The bride and the groom at a Hindu wedding in Kathmandu. The bride usually sits with her head covered while the Brahmin priests pray for the gods' blessings.

DOMESTIC ARCHITECTURE

Housing style in Nepal varies according to ethnic group and regional climate. Many people in the Terai build their homes on stilts and keep their animals below the house. Living above the ground gives them some protection from snakes, animals, and mosquitoes. It is also much cooler and breezier. Every house has a separate compound.

Higher up in the hills, where there are fewer snakes and winters are colder, houses are more solid, with thick stone walls and thatched or slate-tile roofs. Windows are small, without glass panes. There is no chimney for the fire. Houses are built close together, and two or three homes may share a compound.

In the high Himalayan region, people live on the second floor, such as the people in the Terai, but they do it as protection from the cold. Their homes often share a wall with a neighbor's, as homes built together stand a better chance of keeping the cold out. Animals live beneath the house, and their body heat helps to warm the rooms above. The houses are built of stone and wood, with wooden roof shingles weighed down by heavy stones.

A view of the nested houses of Phu from above Nar-Phu in the Annapurna region. Houses in the Himalayas are usually built stacked on top of each other and close together in order to retain heat and keep out the cold.

THE HEARTH

Each ethnic group places special importance on the hearth and cooking area. A non-Brahmin should never enter the cooking area in a Brahmin house. To do so would pollute the area, and a religious "cleansing" ceremony would have to be performed.

A Brahmin male must take off his clothes and wrap a length of white cloth called a *dhoti* (DHOH-tee) around himself before he steps into the hearth area to eat. In the Middle Hills and Himalayas, though, a guest will immediately be given the best seat by the hearth—on the right side, near the back wall of the hearth.

Most social activity in Nepal takes place around the fire—usually an open pit with an iron tripod where pots are placed. Nepalese people have great respect for the hearth, and they are careful not to throw anything that could be considered "unclean" into it.

A TYPICAL DAY IN THE VILLAGE

Work in the village begins before the roosters crow. There is wood to be gathered, fodder to be cut, and water to be fetched. Water may come from a nearby well or from a stream or tap over an hour's walk away. As the forests disappear, water is quickly disappearing too, and people have to walk farther and farther for both fuel and water.

The fire is lit and cooking starts as soon as the household stirs. There may be tea with sugar for breakfast, but probably not every morning. Most people eat rice or *derdho* (DAIR-dhoh)—a mixture of millet, corn, and wheat flour boiled into a thick paste. To go with this, there may be lentil soup and some vegetable curry (potato is most common), or just vegetables with broth. If the family cow or water buffalo has a calf, there may be milk or yogurt.

As food is not always readily available, the hearth is an important part of the traditional Nepali household. Especially in the northern hills, the heart is the center of the house and guests are asked to sit by the fire as soon as they arrive.

After breakfast, some children go to school, while others help out in the fields or at home. School starts at 10 A.M. Whether it is farm work, grazing cattle, or getting wood or water, nearly everything is done manually. After school, children may play or join their parents at work.

It is estimated that more than a third of Nepalese children aged between 5 and 14 years old work in family agricultural pursuits or are hired out as laborers. Nepali law prohibits children under the age of 14 from working but if the family is poor they often have little choice.

Villagers use the sun, not watches or clocks, to tell time. As the sun begins to set, everyone gathers around the fire. Light may come from a tiny kerosene lamp or just from the fire. After eating dinner (probably *derdho* again), the family gathers to talk until everyone goes to sleep.

Nepalese women are an unseen economic force. Women carry out many cottage industries, such as spinning, weaving, and knitting.

A TYPICAL DAY IN TOWN

Nepalese living in towns are also early risers. Nothing tastes better than a steaming glass of Nepali milk tea on a cold morning. Water may be available in the house or have to be fetched from a nearby tap. The mother starts working right away because it can take two hours to cook on her single-burner kerosene stove. She prepares a meal of rice, lentil soup, vegetable curry, and maybe milk or yogurt. Meanwhile, the children get ready for school.

The father then goes to his shop or office, and the mother begins her housework. If the parents can afford it, they send their children to private English schools. The school "bus" may be anything from a rickshaw to a rickety old van.

The mother washes the dishes and clothes at the nearest communal tap and then goes to the market to buy vegetables and other food items for the day, since there is no refrigerator to store a week's groceries. After school, the children play, study, or maybe go see the new Indian movie in town—the cheap seats cost only about $0.05.

The father finishes his work at 5 P.M. and makes his way home slowly. He talks to friends, maybe over a cup of tea or local liquor, and stops at the newsstand to browse through the latest books and magazines. When he comes home, he checks his children's homework. In each room candles are always handy, in case there is a blackout.

The evening meal is served late, at around 8 P.M. or later, and everyone goes to bed soon afterward.

In the cities, some girls from middle-income families are sent to English schools. But after completing their studies, they are still expected to marry and be traditional housewives.

WOMEN IN NEPAL

Surveys show that women do more than 70 percent of the work in the village, such as fetching water, fodder, and firewood, as well as hoeing, weeding, and harvesting crops. They use only basic tools. Work is still mostly done by hand and everything is carried on a person's back.

A new bride usually lives with her husband's family and must earn the respect of her in-laws through hard work at home and in the fields. Although life is difficult for Nepalese women, divorce is rare.

Women in Nepal have almost no decision-making power. Women in caste Hindu homes, in particular, are powerless. Women in Bhote families are able to hold power at home because the men are away on trading trips most of the time. Women in the hill groups are somewhere in-between.

Sons are preferred over daughters, as families must bear large expenses, including in some cases a large dowry, when a daughter marries. But as girls are needed to work in the fields, they are considered both a burden as well as a source of labor. Although the government is trying to improve the condition of women, they are still discriminated against in many areas of Nepalese life.

HEALTH CARE

One out of 25 children in Nepal dies before the age of 1. Five out of every 100 children die before the age of 5, and 49 percent of children under 5 are malnourished. Nepalese families often want many children, as they do not expect all of their children to survive to adulthood.

Many of Nepal's health problems are caused by poor hygiene and sanitation facilities. Few houses have toilets. Instead, people use the nearby fields or streams. Diseases spread easily in this way. Leading causes of child mortality include diarrhea, acute respiratory infection, and malaria. Recent calculations indicate that about 3,000 children under the age of 5 die each year from diarrheal diseases and a further 13,000 from acute respiratory infections.

The government is trying to build a hospital in every district and a health post in every village committee. Still, it takes hours to travel to the health post and days to reach the hospital. Even after people arrive at the hospital, doctors and medicine may not be available, the result of Nepal's poor transportation and communication systems.

A nurse attaches a monitor to a baby in a rural hospital in Kalikot. Lines are long at Nepal's free health clinics. After walking for several hours with their babies in their arms, mothers must wait a long time for their turn.

Whenever they fall sick, many Nepalese still rely on traditional faith healers, called *jankri* (JAHN-kree). The *jankri* supposedly removes the cause of the illness from the person, often by going into a trance while beating on a drum. Some *jankri* have a great deal of knowledge about medicinal plants and are able to mix herbal medicines to treat illnesses.

Young boys having lessons in a village school in Jayamangala.

EDUCATION

There are very few schools in Nepal's rural areas. Students must walk, and in certain areas, it may take them up to two hours to reach school. Lessons are conducted outdoors. Classrooms are used only when necessary, as they are dark and cold because of the lack of electricity. Few textbooks are available, so students are taught to memorize their lessons.

Nepal's literacy rate is 60 percent. Considering the fact that in the 1950s the literacy rate was only 5 percent, the rate has improved a great deal. Schools, teachers, and textbooks are in short supply. More than 85 percent of children enroll in primary school but roughly 40 percent end up dropping out. Less than 50 percent of children attend secondary school.

When Nepalese meet or leave each other, they join their hands in front of them in a prayer-like gesture and say namaste *(neh-MEHS-tay), or sometimes* namaskar *(neh-MEHS-kahr). These phrases are derived from Sanskrit words and literally mean "I bow to you."*

Himalayan people drape a thin white scarf called a khata *(KAH-tah) around the neck of someone they want to show respect to or of someone leaving on a trip.*

Nepalese seldom say dhanyabad *(DHAHN-yah-bahd), meaning "thank you." People do not open a present when it is given. To avoid any chance of embarrassing anyone, they open it in private.*

The feet are considered the dirtiest part of the body, while the head is considered the most sacred. A Nepalese will never step over a person. If a Nepalese touches a person with their feet by accident, they will immediately reach down, touch your feet, and then touch their own head as if to say, "I am sorry. Your feet are higher than my head."

Objects should be passed with the right hand. As the left hand is used to clean oneself after using the toilet, it is considered unclean.

DEATH

Death is treated in different ways in different cultures. Hindus cremate the body by the banks of the nearest river. They then pick out a small piece of bone and throw the ashes in the river. They believe that the ashes will eventually reach the sacred waters of the Ganges River in India.

Among hill groups, the Magar and Tamang also cremate their dead, but on top of a hill. The Gurung either cremate or bury their dead. A priest decides which one it should be, based on the position of the stars at the time of the person's death.

Almost every group in Nepal has elaborate ceremonies to mark the first death anniversary. During this ceremony, the family of the dead person gives a large feast for the entire village.

Wood is scarce in the Himalayan region, and so cremation is difficult. Often the land is also too rocky for digging graves. Some groups who live in these remote areas take the dead body to a high place, cut it up in pieces, throw it in a river or leave it for vultures.

Men preparing a funeral pyre at a cremation ceremony in Pashupatinath, the most sacred temple in Nepal. Hindus believe in cremating their dead and then scattering the ashes in a river.

INTERNET LINKS

www.guru.com.np/belbibha.htm

Website with information on the religions, festivals, and culture of Nepal, including a link to information on the Bel Bibaha festival.

www.news.bbc.co.uk/2/shared/spl/hi/picture_gallery/05/south_asia_nepal_village_life/html/6.stm

This website has a link to a series of photos with detailed captions entitled In Pictures: Nepal village life.

www.nepalfreed.org/index.html

Nepal FREED is an NGO based in Nepal and aims to assist in furthering education for children in Nepal. The website has information on Nepal and a link to a comprehensive set of images.

www.unicef.org/nepal/Child_Poverty-layout.pdf

The UNICEF website has a link to a 2010 report on Nepal entitled Child Poverty and Disparity in Nepal.

RELIGION

Many Hindus pay their respects to this image of Kala Bhairab, also known as the "Black Shiva," located in the Durbar Square of Kathmandu.

ACCORDING TO A recent estimate, Nepal's population is about 81 percent Hindu, 11 percent Buddhist, and 4.5 percent Muslim. The rest of the population belongs to other religions. In everyday life, though, the line between Hinduism and Buddhism is far from clear. Many Nepalese follow both religions.

Hinduism, in particular, is a part of everyday life in Nepal, as it is integrated into daily routines such as shopping or going to work. Because the Buddha is considered a form of the Hindu god Vishnu, the

A Tibetan woman spinning the prayer wheels at Boudhanath, one of the holiest Buddhist sites in Kathmandu. These wheels are meant to help those who are unable to read and recite the Pali scriptures of Buddhism to gain blessings.

8

In Nepal religion is a complex mixture of traditions, faiths, festivals, and doctrines, which have been handed down from generation to generation and permeated every level of Nepalese society. It is an intermingling of Hinduism, Buddhism, and other beliefs.

Buddha's teachings are well known and have great influence even among Nepalese Hindus.

HINDUISM

Hinduism, the oldest living faith in the world, does not have an identifiable founder. There is no governing or regulating body, and there is no specific dogma that spells out what a Hindu should believe.

Hindus define their beliefs in a collection of philosophical writings called the Vedas, which are 1,008 hymns and revelations of saints and seers. The Vedas were first recorded more than 1,000 years ago.

Hinduism embraces many beliefs, so many, in fact, that some beliefs directly contradict others. According to Hindu philosophy, there is more than one righteous path to understand the mysteries of life. The individual's capacities, attitudes, and requirements determine their beliefs. To Hindus, all religions lead to the same end. Hindus may even embrace other religions without ceasing to be Hindus.

A sculpture of the Hindu god Vishnu, known as the "Preserver of the Universe," along with Lakshmi and Garuda at the Changu Narayana temple.

Hindus believe in reincarnation, or rebirth after death, and moving up or down a universal ladder. Their actions in this life determine their next life. If they perform bad deeds in this lifetime, they may be reborn into a lower caste, as animals, or even as insects.

If they do great good in this life, earning much *dharma* (DHARH-mah), or merit, then their next life will be enriched. After living thousands of lives, they may be able to go to heaven, released from the cycle of life and death at last.

To Hindus, people's condition in this world and the things that happen in their lives are part of their *karma* (KAHR-mah), or destiny. Therefore,

HINDU GODS

One Hindu text states that there are 300 million gods, and Hindus actively worship hundreds. But three stand out: Brahma the Creator, Vishnu the Preserver, and Shiva the Destroyer. These three gods combine to become Brahman, the ultimate divinity found in everything.

A god may be called by a dozen different names and may manifest itself in several different forms. Vishnu, for example, has 10 different forms, including a lion, a dwarf, the Hindu hero Krishna, and even the Buddha.

Shiva, with more than 108 different names, is the god most worshiped in Nepal. Known as the Destroyer, he is also called the "bright or happy one," and is honored as Lord of the Dance. He is often pictured as an ascetic, his body smeared with ashes and wrapped in a leopard skin, wandering far and wide or meditating at his home on Mount Kailash in Tibet. It is believed that the waters of the Ganges River spring from the tall pile of hair on his head.

Ganesh, Shiva's son, is one of the most popular gods. His father cut off his head by mistake and, to appease his wife, swore to replace it with the first living thing he found—

which turned out to be an elephant. With his elephant head and roly-poly body, Ganesh does not look like a typical immortal. Still, he is the god most people first turn to with their requests. He is revered as the god of wisdom and the deity for deciding between failure and success.

Durga is one of the representations of Shiva's wife, Parbati. People worship Durga for her victory over a demon during the festival of Dashain (dah-SIGH). Laxmi, the goddess of wealth and prosperity, is appealed to during the festival of Tihar (TEE-hahr). Saraswati, the goddess of wisdom and Brahman's consort, is usually portrayed riding a swan and playing a sitar, an Indian lute with a long neck. Indra, the god of rain, is prayed to during the monsoons.

it does no good to feel anger and rebel against *karma*. *Karma* must be accepted and borne. This attitude of tolerance helps Nepalese Hindus bear their poverty, but it may also diminish their motivation for change.

BUDDHISM

The Buddha's real name was Siddhartha Gautama. The name Buddha is an honorary title meaning "enlightened one." Siddhartha was born around 623 B.C. in Lumbini, which is now part of Nepal's Terai. Born into a rich, perhaps noble, family, he lived a life of luxury and ease in several palaces.

Being curious about life, he made several secret trips outside the palace. Shocked by the pain, death, and suffering of the common people, he decided to renounce everything in his life, including his wife and son, to try to understand what he had seen.

For the next six years, he wandered from place to place. He meditated and searched for the answers to life. Finally realizing them, he became spiritually enlightened. Henceforth known as Lord Buddha he began to preach the Four Noble Truths. According to this doctrine people suffer because of their attachment to things and people; the root of all the problems is desire. These desires, all problems and sufferings, can be eliminated by following the "eightfold path"—right views, right intent, right speech, right conduct, right livelihood, right effort, right mindfulness, and right meditation. For the rest of his life he walked with a group of disciples, talking with anyone who listened or asked him about the meaning of life and spreading his message. He died at Bodh Gaya in present-day India.

Considered to be the oldest temple in Nepal, the ancient temple of Changu Narayan in Bhaktapur houses magnificent art works in metal and wood, and is one of the finest examples of Nepalese architecture.

BUDDHIST DOCTRINE All Buddhists believe that life is based on a cycle of birth, death, and rebirth. One's rebirth depends on one's karma, or the end result of one's actions, words, and thoughts in a lifetime. A Buddhist's goal is to break the cycle of rebirth by living a life of detachment from the desires of this world. If this is done, a person attains Nirvana, or release from the cycle of life and death. Several Buddhist schools have evolved since the Buddha's death. The Mahayana school has influenced Tibet, Nepal, and northern Asia. The Theravada school is followed in Sri Lanka and Southeast Asia. One important difference between the two schools is that in Theravada philosophy believers are only concerned with their own release from the cycle. The Mahayana tradition dictates that those who achieve enlightenment must "go back" and help others do the same.

An ornately decorated Buddha sculpture at the Kopan Monastery in Kathmandu.

FOLK BELIEFS

The Nepalese have customs, superstitions, and rituals, both large and small, that cover almost all aspects of everyday life. Because of Nepal's great cultural diversity, customs that are important or offensive to one culture may mean nothing to another. Here are some customs and beliefs:

- *Never blow out a light with your breath; wave something, even just your hand, to fan out the flame.*

- *After lighting a lamp or just switching on an electric light for the first time that day, a Nepalese will make a namaste gesture (below) toward the light.*

- *Fresh water should be fetched every morning; water that stands overnight is considered no longer clean.*

- *Before serving food, Nepalese will place a little rice in the fire as an offering to the gods.*

- *When you see a baby for the first time, give some money (a rupee or a few coins) to guarantee their future prosperity.*

- *If a bee hovers near you, good fortune is coming.*

The Nepalese travel often, and have various beliefs about travel:

- *If your feet itch, you will be traveling soon.*

- *Some people take a betel nut, a coin, and some rice wrapped in a cloth to ensure a safe trip.*

- *It is unlucky to start a journey on a Tuesday.*

- *It is unlucky to leave under a new moon.*

- *A large jug full of water on each side of the doorway ensures a safe trip.*

- *Try not to come back home on a Saturday.*

Mothers threaten their naughty children with "a foreigner will come and eat you!" But the Nepalese already had enough strange creatures in their culture even before the arrival of foreigners:

- *A jhumi (JHYOO-mi) will grab you and lead you away from your house without your knowledge if you leave early in the morning without telling anyone.*

- *If you meet a beautiful young woman late at night, look at her feet. If they're pointed backward, run! She's a kichikinni (kee-chee-KIN-nee), the spirit of a dead woman.*

- *A mulkatta (mool-KAHT-tah), a dead man's spirit, wanders around headless.*

- *If you wake up, but feel you cannot get up, it is a khya (KHEE-yah) holding you down. If a khya gets upset, it will tickle you to death.*

- *Pret (preht) and pisach (pee-SAHCH), unhappy spirits, wait at crossroads and cremation sites to chase people and make them sick.*

Prayer flags are hung outside Buddhist temples and monasteries. People believe the winds will carry their prayers to heaven.

IN DAILY LIFE

Every morning, the streets of Nepal are filled with people going to the neighborhood shrine for *puja* (POO-jah), or worship. A *puja* is a ceremony in which prayers are offered to the Buddhas to ask for their blessings or request help. People carry trays with colored powder, flower petals, grains of rice, a few sweets, and a small bell. These items are used in worship at the temple.

Many people encountered in the morning will have flower petals in their hair. This is part of *prasad* (prah-SAHD), the blessing received from the gods in return for worshiping them. The mark many people wear on their forehead, the *tika*, is another sign of blessing. It symbolizes the third eye of inner wisdom and vision.

Nepalese believe divinity can be found in everything: in people, in plants and animals, and even in rocks. They would rather build roads around large rocks and trees than remove them, for fear of disturbing their divinity. It is impossible for the Nepalese to separate their daily lives from their religion, as they believe their actions affect this, and the next, life.

Woman gathered for a puja, praying for world peace, in Pokhara.

Hindus worship the cow as their Divine Mother and also as a symbol of fertility. Cow products, such as milk and yogurt, and by-products, such as dung and urine, have special religious significance. A Hindu would never think of killing a cow or eating beef. In Nepal, cows wander loose everywhere. They have good reason to feel safe: the penalty for killing a cow, even by accident, can be up to 20 years in jail.

A Brahmin priest gives a *tika* (TEE-kah) to a lady. The *tika* is a sign of blessing and a symbol of knowledge.

OTHER RELIGIONS

About 4.5 percent of Nepal's population is Muslim. Almost all Muslims live in the western Terai, but there is a small active community in Kathmandu. There is a very small Christian population. In certain remote areas of the Himalayas, Bon, the Tibetan religion prior to Buddhism, is still followed.

In the face of cultural and religious diversity, the Nepalese exercise great tolerance and mutual respect for the beliefs of others. They are proud that religious conflict has never been a problem in Nepal.

INTERNET LINKS

www.kopanmonastery.com/

Official website of the Kopan monastery in Kathmandu. The site contains information on the history of the monastery, monastic life, prayers, and practices.

www.nepalfolklore.org/

Official website of the Nepali Folklore Society.

www.thamel.com/htms/religions.htm

Website with general information on Nepal and a detailed section on religion.

LANGUAGE

Tibetan Mani stones in the Chekhung valley contain inscriptions along the mountain passes to protect those who travel along the precarious path.

9

THERE ARE MORE THAN A dozen languages spoken in Nepal and each language has many dialects. In fact dialects change with almost every ridge you cross. A Tamang from Dhading in central Nepal will have a hard time understanding a Tamang from Taplejung in the east. Because of Nepal's harsh geography, there is little interaction between groups.

The *Ethnologue* is an encyclopedia reference work cataloging all of the world's known languages. The number of individual languages and dialects listed for Nepal is 126. Of those, 124 are living languages and two have no known speakers.

Students studying English at the Manjughoksha Academy in Bodhnath in Kathmandu.

Men gather to chat or read newspapers at a store along the streets of Kathmandu.

Nepali is the national language, and it is used by people from different groups to speak to one another. Nepali is an Indo-Aryan language and has many similarities to the grammar and vocabulary of Hindi, spoken in northern India. Nepali and Hindi share the same script.

NEPALI

Nepali first started to be used in writing in the 12th century. It is written using the Devanagari alphabet that developed from the *Brahmi* script in the 11th century. Nepali sentence structure is very different from English construction. The usual order is subject-object-verb. There are "markers" to identify the words that are the subject, object, or indirect object. The marker for the subject is -le; for an indirect object the marker is -laai. For example:

Ramle Sitalaai paani diyo.
Ram to Sita water gave.
(Ram gave water to Sita.)

There are two different verbs that share the function of the English verb "to be." One form is used when describing something that is so at that moment, while the other is used for a permanent state of being.

Nepali uses sounds nonexistent in English. For example, there are two "d" sounds. Nepali also uses several aspirated sounds, almost like an extra "h" added to a sound, such as "ka" and "kha." The difference in pronunciation is very difficult for a non-Nepalese to hear and pick up.

LANGUAGE AS ETIQUETTE

The Nepali language can be very formal and polite. The words one uses will change according to whether one is talking to a friend, a shopkeeper, one's parents, or a high official. There is even a separate vocabulary for speaking to the royal family.

The words used when talking to people depend on their status relative to the speaker. "Higher" words are used with people one should show respect

Book shops in Nepal are mainly for tourists. Books are a luxury as many Nepalese are either illiterate or unable to afford them.

to and "lower" words with people who should show respect to the speaker. This means that children will use one grammatical form to ask their parents a question; the parents, in turn, will use another form in reply.

The same is the case at work. Bosses will use words and forms that will leave no doubt in their subordinates' minds as to who is the boss. With their own superiors, on the other hand, bosses will use words that show respect.

WRITING

The Devanagari script is very old. It is the same script used to write Hindi, Marathi, and the ancient languages Sanskrit and Prakrit. Each character represents a unique sound, not a letter. Words are formed by joining the characters with a line across the top. The Nepalese write below the line on lined paper.

Nepal is a nation of linguists. It is not uncommon for even young children to speak two or three different languages. Most children start out speaking their own group's language at home, then learn Nepali in school. They usually pick up Hindi as they grow up. In school, they also study English.

A man reading a text written in Nepali.

OTHER LANGUAGES

The hill groups and Bhotes speak Tibeto-Burmese languages. These languages are slightly similar to Chinese in that they are monosyllabic and tonal. To speak correctly, the right stress and tone, either rising or falling, must be used. The same syllable may have several meanings based on the stress given to the sound when speaking. The Bhote languages are very close to Tibetan and use the Tibetan script.

Newari, the language of the Newar, is an Indo-European language that has absorbed a great deal of influence from the Tibeto-Burmese languages. It is one of the most difficult languages in the world to learn.

People in the Terai speak a great number of Indo-European languages. After Nepali, the two most widely spoken languages are Bhojpuri and Maithili. These languages are classified as an Indo-European language and are very different from Nepali. Although the languages have common roots, a Nepali speaker and a Maithili speaker will have a very difficult time understanding one another.

NEPALI LITERATURE

Twentieth-century Nepalese writers mainly wrote about conditions in Nepalese society.

The majority of monks in Nepal are refugees from Tibet and live in monasteries in Nepal. Young monks also attend daily classes in a school setting within the monastery.

What is something totally insignificant? It is "a cumin seed on an elephant's trunk."
The Nepalese have all kinds of proverbs and sayings that reflect the world they live in.
Some of them are easy for us to understand, while others require a little reflection:

- *He can't face a live tiger, but he'll pull the whiskers off a dead one.*
- *He couldn't see a buffalo on himself, but he'll find a louse on someone else.*
- *Too many cats kill no mice.*
- *If you need a drink, you have to find a spring.*
- *Give someone a drink, but don't show them the spring.*
- *No one sits by a burnt-out fire.*
- *A knot tied with a laugh is untied with tears.*
- *Dress according to the land you are in.*
- *It takes a hundred more lies to hide the first.*
- *The sun can't be covered with your hand.*
- *The carpenter's staircase is broken.*
- *The elephant went through, but its tail was caught.*

One of the 20th century's most famous writers was Bal Krishna Sama (1903—81). Born to a rich, aristocratic Rana family, he was appalled by the abuses committed by the Rana regime against the common Nepalese people. He changed his title to *sama*, which means "equal," as a way of bridging the gap between his privileged status and that of the rest of the Nepalese population. His novels, poetry, and essays draw from both Sanskrit and English literary traditions.

A contemporary of Sama, Poet Laksmi Prasad Devkota (1909—59) was also influenced by the literary traditions of the West, particularly poetry, tragic drama, and the short story.

Bhupi Sherchan (1936—89) is one of the most popular and widely read Nepali poets in recent years. His poems are written in simple Nepali and they address issues crucial to all Nepalese, not just to the educated elite. His collection of 42 prose poems entitled "A Blind Man on a Revolving Chair" (*Ghumne Mechmathi Andho Manche*) was published in 1969 and awarded the Sajha Puraskar prize. This collection has become one of the most influential and acclaimed collections of Nepali poetry.

Tibetan script on blue painted rocks in front of a Buddhist monastery in Annapurna.

INTERNET LINKS

www.publishing.cdlib.org/ucpressebooks/

The official website of UCP includes a section entitled "Himalaya Voices" that includes biographies of Nepali poets and writers.

www.ethnologue.com/home.asp

This website has a link to a section on Nepal listing all languages spoken and a description of each.

www.omniglot.com/writing/nepali.htm

Online encyclopedia of writing systems and languages, including Nepali and the Devanagari alphabet.

ARTS

Classical dancers in their traditional costumes in Nepal.

N KATHMANDU IT IS EASY to walk past a 1,000-year-old statue without even noticing it. As daily life swirls around, the Nepalese treat masterpieces in wood, stone, metal, and brick with the casualness of an old friend. It may be hard for Westerners, used to hushed, pristine museums, to understand. But for the Nepalese, great works of art are as much a part of daily life as the morning cup of tea.

Nepalese art is unique and expressions of art are evident in the daily practice of religion. Nepalese pagodas, temples, and stupas represent a rich repository of metal work, wood carving, terracotta, and stone sculpture. The major art forms of Nepal are found in architecture, pottery, painting, and bronze figures.

The *garuda* (gah-ROO-da) is a mythical bird from the religious drama the *Ramayana*. Garuda sculptures can be found in other Asian countries of Hindu influence, though the sculptures do not look exactly alike.

To Nepalese, their art is not to be locked away and viewed from a distance on special occasions; it is an inherent part of their daily environment, to be touched, sat on, worshiped, or even used to entertain little children.

Nepal's greatest fine arts are found in the forms of sculpture and architecture. There is almost no secular art. Most Nepali art is generated for worshiping in the two great religious traditions that shape so much of life in the country—Hinduism and Buddhism.

Nepali art is mostly anonymous. We know the names of the patrons who commissioned the works, but not the names of the artists and craftsmen who executed them.

This is not the case with popular music. Songwriters are household names, and the favorite subject by far is romance. Nepalese children are brought up to sing and dance without being self-conscious. The ability to sing with wit and dance with grace often helps adult Nepalese attract and win the heart of that special someone.

In a country largely free of television and radio, the Nepalese still rely on each other's artistic talent for entertainment.

Buddhist monks playing religious music at a ceremony in the monastery.

MUSIC

The Nepalese love music. Walk through any village and you are bound to hear the voice of someone singing, the lilting sound of a flute, or the catchy rhythm of a drum. Radios are becoming more common, but still, in most places in Nepal, if you want to hear music, you must play it yourself.

A wedding would not be a wedding in Nepal without a band announcing the approach of the wedding party. In the far west the band consists mostly of drummers. In the Middle Hills people play the *shehnai* (shah-NYE), a double-reed conical oboe-like instrument, and big horns that curve back and over. In the cities, bands with Western instruments blast out Western and Hindi pop songs in a style that is half-polka, half-Dixieland, and all fun.

The hymns and religious songs sung at temples are accompanied by drums, large and tiny cymbals, flutes, and harmoniums. In Buddhist monasteries high in the Himalayas, monks stand on rooftops to play huge horns that are 10 to 15 feet (3 to 4.5 m) long. Their low bass rumble echoes through the high mountain valleys and can be heard for miles.

Panche Baja which translates literally as "five musical instruments" is a group of five musical instruments that are played at certain auspicious occasions such as wedding celebrations. A small band of five people perform using three different drums, a *shehnai*, and cymbals.

SONG

Singing is almost a national sport in Nepal. A singing competition is always one of the main attractions at festivals in the Middle Hills.

There are two teams—a boys' team and a girls' team. One side sings a short verse, asking rhetorical questions, criticizing the other team's song or dress or telling a story. As one team sings, the other must think up a wittier and more poetic reply. Onlookers offer judgments. Highest marks go to the wittiest verses. The singing may go back and forth all night without a winner. It may end with an agreement to continue the competition at the same place, same time, the following year.

One of the great traditions of Nepali music, and one that is fast disappearing, is *gaini* (GUY-nee). *Gaini* are wandering musicians who travel from town to town and sing for their supper. They are *Gandharbas*, a caste of musicians found throughout Nepal. They sing and play the *sarangi*, a wooden fiddle of no fixed size that is held upright. The strings were traditionally made from intestines of goats but nowadays nylon strings are used. The bow is made of horse hair. *Gandharbas* are masters of song and improvisation. *Kharkas* are epic songs about gods, soldiers, or public figures. *Mangal* are sung for good luck and often relate stories of the gods. *Ghatana* songs describe contemporary newsworthy events. *Gaini* make a living from the donations given by the crowd of villagers who gather to listen. Long ago, *gaini* families traveled together, the children learning the songs at their father's knee.

A *gaini* in Kathmandu sings with a *sarangi*, a traditional violin-like folk instrument made from a single piece of wood with a hollow frame and dried sheepskin. Due to urbanization, Nepal has seen a massive decline in the tradition.

DRAMA

Traditional dramas retell the two great epics, the *Ramayana* and the *Mahabharata*. These dramas are performed during religious festivals and are sponsored by religious organizations.

Comedy has a long tradition in Nepal, and no drama would be complete without a comic interlude or two, sometimes even three. In recent years comic reviews have toured larger cities and have met with great success.

The biggest comedy event of the year occurs during the Gai Jatra festival. The festival of cows is one of the most popular festivals of Nepal. Celebrated in Kathmandu, it is the one day of the year when you can poke fun at anything or anybody, even big and powerful public figures. There are no rules; anything can be said and no one can take offense. The results are uproarious.

Nepal has a growing modern drama movement. Street drama is very popular and highly influential. The plots are mainly concerned with social issues and the new problems confronting Nepal's increasingly urban, Western-influenced population—youthful alienation, evil schemers, drugs, and even topics such as government corruption and the position of women in

Nepalese children, dressed in "cow costumes," take part in a procession for Gai Jatra (Cow Festival) in Kathmandu. Families who have lost a relative during the year parade a cow, a sacred animal supposed to help the departed soul to enter the afterlife, through the city.

society. The language is uncomplicated and the people can easily relate to the characters and grasp the story line of the play.

On the annual Earthquake Safety Day the National Society for Earthquake Technology (NSET) in Nepal organizes annual street dramas on the subject of earthquakes. These productions educate people on safety precautions, risk reduction, and preparedness. The subject is a sensitive one in Nepal as the country is prone to earthquakes. The Street Talent Concern Nepal performed a street drama on the subject of human immunodeficiency virus infection/acquired immunodeficiency syndrome (HIV/AIDS), educating people on this sensitive issue.

DANCE

Religious dances are very common in Nepal. The dancers wear elaborate costumes and huge masks and headdresses. Their dances depict the struggles and triumphs of the gods over demons. Religious dancers walk through the streets and dance at the temples and the old palace during the Indra Jatra (IN-drah JAH-trah) festival. Lakhe Dance is a typical Newari musical play. This ancient dance of the devil captures the tradition of the Newar community and is a celebration of mythological stories and tradition.

According to tradition, Lakhe is a demon who, as penance for his wicked ways while an ordinary man, is charged with fighting other demons and keeping them away from Kathmandu.

Buddhists have a strong tradition of religious dances. Twice a year, in the Mount Everest area, the Sherpas hold a three-day epic dance reenacting the triumph of Buddhism over the old Bon religion. People from all over the world come to see the elaborate costumes and masks and the elegant, controlled energy of the dancers.

Every ethnic group in Nepal has its own style of folk dancing. Himalayan people put their arms around each other's shoulders and form a sort of chorus line. Rai and Limbu hold hands (both men and women) and dance slowly in a circle.

In caste Hindu culture, men and women rarely dance together; women rarely dance at all. Traditionally one or two men will dance surrounded by a close circle of people singing, clapping, and urging the swirling dancers on.

LITERATURE

Nepal is a nation of poets. Several poetry competitions are held each year. These competitions are often broadcast on the radio, and with the start of television broadcasting in some areas in the late 1980s, the finals are now shown on the small screen as well.

Birthdays of most famous poets are celebrated with parades and recitations of their poems. Laksmi Prasad Devkota (1909—59) is considered

A Tibetan dance group in Nepal.

THE *MAHABHARATA* AND THE *RAMAYANA*

These Hindu epics combine the teachings of the Vedas with great stories and legends. They have been entertaining and teaching children and adults alike for thousands of years. Present-day Nepalese children can still recount the adventures of their favorite heroes.

Like the Greek Iliad, *the stories have a basis in both myth and history, with the gods and goddesses playing an active role in the affairs of people. The* Mahabharata *recounts the heroic struggle of five brothers, the* Pandavas, *against their 100 evil cousins, the* Kauravas. *Within the* Mahabharata, *the Bhagavad Gita (Song of God) presents the essence of Hinduism.*

The Ramayana *centers on the adventures of the great hero Ram, his wife Sita, and his brother Lakshmana. Sita is kidnapped by the terrible demon Ravana. After much searching, Ram's messenger and favorite general, the monkey king Hanuman, finds her on the island of Sri Lanka. Following a terrific battle, Ram finally kills the demon and rescues Sita with Hanuman's help (right).*

Nepal figures in both epics. The great Nepalese king Yalambar is killed in the Mahabharata's *climactic battle. In the* Ramayana, *Ram wins Sita's hand in marriage in a competition in Sita's home, Janakpur, in Nepal's Terai.*

one of Nepal's greatest poets. He began to write poetry at a very young age and is considered to be the creator of romanticism. Devkota wrote stories, plays, novels, songs, short poems, and prose. He had command of the Nepali, Sanskrit, Hindi, and English languages. His most famous work *Muna-Madan* is the highest selling book ever in Nepal.

Brahmins, members of the religious caste, sometimes privately publish a booklet of long, original poems. They recite their poems in public, singing them to a simple melody, and sell the booklets to the audience gathered around them. These poems are usually religious sermons, using a story to illustrate Hindu scriptures.

PAINTING

There are two main painting traditions in Nepal, one with roots in the south and the other found in the north. Paintings are also mainly devoted to religious themes.

A religious painting on the wall of Pashupatinath Temple in Kathmandu.

The Buddhist "wheel of life" is painted in the style of Tibetan Buddhist scrolls called *thangka*. This is found in the Kopan monastery in Bhaktapur.

Newari paintings from as far back as the 11th century show southern influences. These paintings are miniatures used to illustrate manuscripts, and the style is derived from Indian art. By the 15th century, Brahmanic manuscripts were being beautifully decorated with miniatures done in a style similar to India's *pahari* (pah-HAH-ree) art. The painters were *Chitrakars* (CHEE-trah-kerhs), meaning they belonged to the painter caste in the rigid caste system in effect under the Malla kings.

Chitrakars also painted delicate frescoes in temples and palaces and are renowned for their *paubha* (POW-bah) paintings on religious scrolls. Around the 14th century, Nepalese artists traveled to Tibet and across Central Asia and brought a new art form back to Nepal. Inspired by Tibetan scroll paintings called *thangka* (TAHNG-kah), which depict the Buddha and other Buddhist themes such as the "wheel of life," Nepalese painters began to work on scrolls that were rich in color, elaborate in design, and extremely detailed. The first Newar artist to travel abroad was Bhaju Man, a painter of the *Chitrakar* caste. He formed part of the group traveling with Maharaja Jang Bahadur Rana on his journey to England and France in 1850. This became a turning point for Nepalese artists who had previously remained anonymous because their religious works had not been judged as art but as merit earned toward attaining Nirvana. The idea of art was reevaluated in Nepal, away from art motivated by myth and religion toward works that served personal edification and was purely aesthetic in nature.

Traditionally the *Chitrakars* were given exclusive rights to paint and draw in certain houses and palaces, and to this day they paint religious pictures and create ritual masks and ceremonial vessels for religious events and festivals.

SCULPTURE

Nepalese sculpture reached its peak during the reign of the Malla kings from the 15th to the 17th centuries. Most of the carvings were made by Newar craftsmen to decorate palaces and temples. Nepal boasts stone sculpture from the sixth century, and the wooden figures on some of the temples are more than 900 years old. Nepalese sculptors worked in many media, including wood, stone, metal (usually brass), and terracotta. But they liked best to work with metal. They used the lost wax method, making a wax model to make a clay mold, both of which were destroyed when the statue was made. Another popular technique used a hammer and chisel to tap and pound a design into a sheet of metal, usually copper.

Both these methods are still in use today. Visitors walking down the streets of Patan will hear the clinking sound of craftsmen's hammers tapping on metal.

Brightly painted sculptures decorate a Tibetan temple in Nepal.

At the end of the 13th century, a master Nepalese architect, known today as Arniko, traveled north at the invitation of the Mongol emperor Kublai Khan who wanted to build a golden stupa in Lhasa. As he and his team of 24 assistants completed several projects, Arniko's reputation spread and came to the attention of the Ming emperor of China. Arniko joined the court of the emperor, who gave him the title of Duke of Liang as an honor. The white pagoda or the Pai Taa Sze still stands in Beijing today. The style of pagodas seen today all throughout East Asia owes its origins to this remarkable and little-known man.

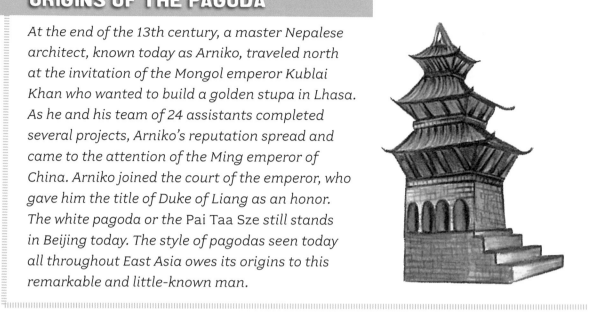

ARCHITECTURE

Religious architecture is Nepal's main contribution to world art. The Kathmandu Valley is designated a world heritage site by the United Nations Educational, Scientific and Cultural Organization (UNESCO). No other place in the world can boast so many landmarks in such a small area. Lumbini, the birthplace of Lord Buddha, was inscribed on the world heritage list in 1997. The cultural heritage of the Kathmandu Valley, inscribed in 1979, is illustrated by seven groups of monuments and buildings. These display the complete range of historic and artistic achievements for which the Kathmandu Valley is famous. The seven sites include the Durbar Squares of Hanuman Dhoka (Kathmandu), Patan, and Bhaktapur, the Buddhist stupas of Swayambhu and Boudhanath, and the Hindu temples of Pashupati and Changu Narayan.

Much of Nepal's distinctive architecture was the work of Newar artisans during the 17th and 18th centuries when craftsmen were paid from the state treasury. They built with brick, wood, and stone, so today the palace squares remain much as they were centuries ago. Most of these buildings are located in the Durbar Squares of Bhaktapur, Kathmandu, and Patan.

In the 19th and 20th centuries, the Rana prime ministers filled Kathmandu with huge, European-style palaces. The largest of these palaces have been made into government offices and hotels.

In the Buddhist areas of Nepal, structures that are half-sculpture, half-architecture, called stupas, can be found. Two of the largest are located at Boudhanath and Swayambhu in the Kathmandu Valley.

INTERNET LINKS

www.sacred-texts.com/hin/dutt/

This website contains an abridged verse translation of the two longest epic poems in world literature, the Ramayana and the Mahabharata.

www.nset.org.np/nset/php/about.php

This website contains information about earthquakes in Nepal. One of its objectives is to raise awareness among the people on the options available to reduce earthquake disasters. It has many links including a page of visual clips of street drama productions.

www.artsofnepal.com/paintings/20/newari-pauba.html

Online gallery representing many Nepalese artists in the medium of paintings, prints, and sculptures.

www.carylsherpa.com/

This is the official website of author and photographer Caryl Sherpa, an American who married the Sherpa guide she met while trekking in the Annapurnas.

Opposite: **The Swayambhunath Stupa (Monkey Temple) in Kathmandu. Stupas are Buddhist representations of the universe. The mound represents earth, water, air, and fire. The eyes are those of the Buddha. The third eye is the eye of true knowledge. The nose is the number 1 and represents unity. The 13 rings of the spire are the 13 degrees of knowledge. The ladder to Nirvana is represented by an umbrella-like structure at the top.**

LEISURE

Little girls playing with a skipping rope in Nepal.

LIFE IN NEPAL moves at a slower pace than it does in the United States or Europe. There are no shopping malls, and most stores are a single small room, stocked with the basic necessities.

The state operates two television stations but TV reaches only a small portion of the population in Kathmandu and the Terai area and broadcasts for only a few hours a day. There are over 400 FM licensed radio stations, with only about 300 operational. Parks and sports fields are found in just a few cities. There are dozens of newspapers, but distribution is slow and limited. Other reading material is scarce.

Young boys in Nepal enjoying a game of soccer.

Nepal follows the Hindu Vedic calendar, with Sunday as the first day of the week and Saturday as the rest day. In Kathmandu most international organizations, NGOs, and some private enterprises follow the international trend of a five-day work week.

What do people do when they are not working? Mostly people like to relax and hang out, talking to friends, listening to other people talking to their friends, sipping a cup of milk tea in the village tea shop, and watching people walk by.

Some lie down in a cool, shady spot and take a nap; others just sit under a tree and wait for a friend to come by so that they can exchange the latest village gossip.

MOVIES

Nepalese love to go to the movies. Every large town with access to electricity has a theater of some kind. Most of the movies are imported from India and are in Hindi. Since Hindi is very similar to Nepali, most Nepalese have no problem understanding the dialogue.

Hindi movies can be enjoyed even without understanding the language. The plots are simple and direct, the bad guys are really bad, the heroines are beautiful, and the heroes are almost supermen.

Movies last about three hours and have a little bit of everything in them—tragedy, comedy, action, and spectacular musical numbers—and often switch from one to the other in the space of a few seconds. The seats may be

A cinema hall in Kathmandu. Going to the movies is a favorite pastime. Nepalese will sometimes pay three times the price for tickets to a popular movie on the black market.

backless benches, the theater may be as hot as an oven, and the projector bulb may blow every 10 minutes, but movies are still a great entertainment.

Video is bringing movies to even the most remote villages. Porters will carry a television, a videocassette recorder, and a small generator for days through the hills, turning the school hall of each village into a temporary theater. The entire village will turn out to watch. Many villagers have never been to the movies. At first they may not even understand the images on the screen, but like anywhere else, they quickly become movie fans.

Nepali chess or *bagh-chal*, uses pieces shaped like tigers and goats.

TRADITIONAL PASTIMES AND SPORTS

With no spare money to spend on elaborate equipment, most Nepali games only require what can be recycled from home or the ground.

One of the most popular children's games is *dandi biyo* (DHAHN-dee byoo). The game involves two objects: the *dandi*, which is a long stick, and the *biyo*, which is a short stumpy stick with pointed ends. The *biyo* is placed across a small groove in the ground and flicked up with the *dandi*. The player tries to tap the stick twice while it is still in the air, and then hit it as far as possible. The farthest hit wins.

Kite flying is also popular. Nepali kites have no tails and control is difficult. Once up in the air, kites fight each other. The goal is to use your kite's string to snap the string of your opponent's kite.

Nepal's most famous game, *bagh-chal*, meaning "tigers and goats," is played on a board. The object of the game is for the tigers to eat up all the goats by jumping over them onto an open space or for the goats to trap all the tigers by preventing them from moving. The game is for two players. One opponent plays four tiger pieces and the other plays 20 goat pieces.

Nepal's traditional national sport is *kabaddi* (KAH-bahd-dee), which originated in India. Two teams of boys face each other across a line on the ground. A player from team A rushes across the line and attempts to tag one of the players on team B, while saying "*kabaddi.*" The players on team B try to avoid the tag, but if one of them is tagged, they rush to stop their opponent from recrossing the line. If they can hold him until he runs out of breath and stops yelling "*kabaddi,*" they win; he wins if he recrosses the line. There is a similar game for all-girl teams. National tournaments for both sexes are held every year.

THE *MELA*

Local festivals called *mela* (MAY-lah) are a source of leisure for all Nepalese. *Mela* are religious celebrations, but the atmosphere is more like a carnival. The date of the *mela* is based on the phases of the moon, usually a full moon or new moon, or halfway between. No special activities take place at the *mela.* It is just a time for people to get together and have fun.

Gambling is a regular feature at the mela. Here, the men bet on which way the walnut shells will land when thrown.

Often people will walk for days to go to a good *mela*. At the *mela* people get a chance to see friends from other villages, to eat foods they cannot eat everyday, and to buy clothes or jewelry. Men gamble; women gossip and shop. Young people sing, dance, and court, and small children do not worry about bedtime. Sometimes a porter carries in a videocassette recorder and a generator, and two or three movies will be shown repeatedly for as long as fuel for the generator lasts.

Sadhu busking for alms during the annual mela (festival) at Ridi bazaar in Nepal.

Mela can last from one day to several days. Each community will hold its own *mela*, providing entertainment at intervals throughout the year. *Mela* are usually held near rivers or streams.

INTERNET LINKS

www.boardgamegeek.com/boardgame/315/bagh-chal

Website with information on the rules and strategy of various board games, including the Nepalese game of *Bagh Chal*.

www.nocnepal.org.np/index.php

Official website of the Nepal Olympic Committee.

www.wavemag.com.np/issue/article314.html

This website is an online magazine from Nepal. It includes sections for arts, music, technology, education, and sports. The sports section includes an article entitled "Sticks and Stones," or the game of *dandi biyo*.

FESTIVALS

The Kumari house, a quadrangle Newari structure bearing the most exotic of all wood carvings in the area of Basantapur Durbar Square. The house was built in 1757 during the reign of King Jaya Prakash Malla.

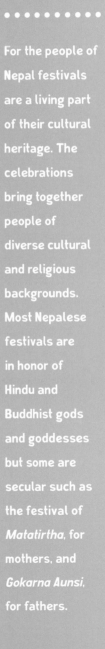

NEPAL HAS DOZENS of festivals. If you include local festivals, it is safe to say that every day of the year there is a festival taking place somewhere in Nepal. Although there are some secular holidays, all the major holidays and festivals are based on religious celebrations.

Many festivals are dedicated to the worship of a god or a goddess. *Shiva Ratri* (SHEE-vah RAH-tree), for example, is dedicated to the Hindu God Shiva. Some festivals have a more human face. *Bhai Tika* (bhye TEE-kah) is the last day of Diwali celebrations in Nepal. It is a festival for brothers

Nepalese observe *Bhai Tika*, during which sisters pay respect to their brothers and wish them a safe and good life on the last day of Tihar.

For the people of Nepal festivals are a living part of their cultural heritage. The celebrations bring together people of diverse cultural and religious backgrounds. Most Nepalese festivals are in honor of Hindu and Buddhist gods and goddesses but some are secular such as the festival of *Matatirtha*, for mothers, and *Gokarna Aunsi*, for fathers.

Festival dates are determined using Nepal's lunar calendar. Thus the dates change every year on the Western calendar.

December to January	Seto Machhendranath
	The holy month of Magh
February to March	Shiva Ratri (Shiva's Night)
	Tribhuvan Jayanti
March to May	Baleju Jatra
	Ghora Jatra
	Biskhet Jatra
	Mother's Day
	Rato Machhendranath
	Buddha Jayanti (Buddha's Birthday)
May to August	Mani Rimdu
	Naga Panchami (Day of the Snakes)
	Janai Purnima
August to September	Gai Jatra
	Krishna Jayanti (Krishna's Birthday)
	Father's Day
	Tij
September to October	Indra Jatra
	Dashain
	Tihar (Festival of Lights)
November to December	Sita Bibha Panchami
	Bala Chaturdasi

and sisters. *Tij* (teej) is celebrated by women only on behalf of their husbands.

Each religious group in Nepal celebrates its own religious holidays; few festivals are observed nationwide. *Dashain*, the biggest Hindu holiday, is not celebrated by Buddhists. *Losar* (LOH-sahr), the New Year's Day and the biggest holiday for the Himalayan people, is not celebrated by the rest of the population. *Indra Jatra* is observed only in the Kathmandu Valley.

In the Himalayan area, most Buddhist monasteries hold annual dance festivals in the monastery's courtyard. Dancers in elaborate costumes and masks enact fables and legends, providing both entertainment and moral education.

Most towns hold one big festival, or *mela*, every year. Overnight small stalls selling food and trinkets spring up in an open field. People walk all day, eat, sing, dance, and gamble all night, then walk back home. The largest *mela* is the *Triveni Mela* held under the full moon in February. More than 100,000 people gather for this one-day fair.

Nepalese devotees crawl under a cow, regarded as an incarnation of the Hindu Goddess of prosperity Laxmi, during the Tihar festival in Kathmandu. Hindus across the country worship cows on the third day of the *Tihar* festival, which commemorates the time when Hindu god Lord Rama achieved victory over Ravana and returned to his kingdom after 14 years in exile.

TIHAR—FESTIVAL OF LIGHTS

Tihar is one of the most dazzling of all Hindu celebrations. There are gifts, decorated houses lit at night, special foods, and even a special nocturnal visitor—Laxmi, the goddess of wealth and good fortune.

Five creatures are worshiped during *Tihar*. On the first day, food is left out for crows. On the second day, dogs are given flower necklaces and *tika* and fed at a banquet. Cows, symbols of Laxmi, are fed, bathed, and garlanded on the third day, and bullocks on the fourth. On the fifth day, the last creatures, people, receive blessings to remain healthy.

At midnight of the third day, Laxmi visits deserving homes. Houses are cleaned and decorated with tinsel and lights. Families prepare to receive Laxmi by painting a path leading from the door to where the home's valuables are placed and adorning it with oil lamps. They place a burning lamp, some flowers, and food for Laxmi beside the valuables table. Children set off fireworks.

The women of the neighborhood go singing from house to house and are rewarded with presents. On the following night it is the men's turn to go out singing.

On the fourth day, homes are lit again. The Newar celebrate their New Year's Day on this day. On the fifth day, men and boys receive the *Bhai Tika*, or "brother's blessing," from their sisters. This blessing is so important that even if a sister has moved far away to another village, men will travel to the sister's home to receive the blessing. If a boy does not have a sister, a relative will act the part. In return for the blessing, the sister receives gifts.

TIJ—FESTIVAL FOR WOMEN

Although it means fasting for at least a day, women in Nepal look forward to the three days of *Tij*. It is their only break from household duties. On the first day the women of the household eat a fine feast, sparing no expense as they must fast on the second day.

During Tihar, *Nepal's cities and towns are ablaze with lights to guide the goddess of wealth to people's homes.*

The fast reenacts Parbati's fast when she prayed that God Shiva would marry her. Shiva did marry her, and in return, Parbati promised that any woman who fasted would be blessed with a good marriage and many children.

All day groups of women gather by rivers and streams. After bathing they dress in their best clothes, usually a bright red sari, and worship Shiva. Then they gather with friends and neighbors to sing and dance into the night.

On the morning of the third day, each woman makes an offering of food to her husband and breaks her fast. A ritual bath ends the festival.

Hundreds of Sadhu Babas will make their way to Pashupatinath temple to celebrate the annual *Shiva Ratri* Festival.

SHIVA RATRI—SHIVA'S NIGHT

Each February, tens of thousands of Nepalese come to the Kathmandu Valley to bathe in the Bagmati River at the point where it flows by Pashupatinath temple. Devotees come from India and all over Nepal on the 14th day of the waning moon.

Long ago, on this date, Shiva is supposed to have spent a whole night here in meditation. He is said to love the spot so much that he returns every year on the same night to meditate. People who spend the night in meditation and then bathe at dawn are supposed to gain the god's favor.

On Shiva's night the woods near the temple become a huge campground, lit with the fires of thousands of pilgrims, chanting and trying to keep warm throughout the night. In February the temperature may be 32°F (0°C) and the water is freezing cold. Bathing is no easy thing to do.

At the first light of dawn, people start bathing in the icy river. They stand in line for hours to pour a little of the river's water over a stone lingam (LING-gum), a fertility symbol representing Shiva.

INDRA JATRA

The *Indra Jatra*, which lasts eight days, is the main festival of the Kathmandu Valley and is celebrated by both Hindus and Buddhists. The festival is named after Lord Indra, the god of rain and also the king of heaven. Long ago, Indra came to the valley to steal some beautiful flowers. He was caught by the people and tied in heavy ropes like a common man. It was not until Indra's mother came to seek him and convinced the people of Indra's true identity that they released him. In return, she gave the people two gifts. She would take to heaven all who died that year and she would give the valley wet, foggy winter mornings to help moisten the crops. During the festival, beautifully costumed and masked dancers wander through Kathmandu, reenacting the search for Indra.

For three nights during the festival, the *Kumari*, the Living Goddess, is carried through the streets in her chariot. Kumari Devi is considered to be an incarnation of the Goddess Taleju. Chariots of Kumari, Ganesha, and Bhairav are carried around the city for three days. According to Hindu belief Ganesha is the son of Shiva and Parvati, and Bhairav is another form of Lord Shiva himself.

The festival of Indra Jatra lasts for eight days with much celebration, singing, dancing, and feasting. Many different traditional dances are performed, with the participants wearing a variety of traditional masks and costumes. People from all over Nepal, mostly those who live within the Kathmandu Valley, gather at the Hanuman Dhoka in Kathmandu.

From the huge mouth of a Bhairav mask flows rice beer, in which a small fish is placed. Drinking this fish guarantees prosperity for the following year.

THE *KUMARI*

The Kumari (koo-MAH-ree) is believed to be the Goddess Kanya Kumari in human form. The Kumari is chosen at the age of about 4 from the Sakya clan of goldsmiths and silversmiths. She becomes a living, breathing goddess—Kumari Devi, a deified young girl. The custom of worshiping a prepubescent girl as the source of supreme power is an old Hindu—Buddhist tradition that continues in Nepal.

Her body must have 32 attributes of perfection and cannot have any flaws or scars. She must identify items known only to the Kumari. Lastly she must walk fearlessly through a dark room filled with men in demon masks and bloody buffalo heads. If she fulfills all of these requirements and can endure the last test, she is the Kumari, the Living Goddess.

The Kumari moves into a palace, where she lives like a queen. She is forbidden to leave except on a few special occasions. Even then, she is carried because her feet must never touch the ground.

She remains the Kumari until she loses blood, either from a cut or on reaching puberty. Then she returns to her own family, an ordinary person again. Many ex-Kumaris find this transition from divinity back to being a mortal very difficult to make. For some, being the Kumari becomes a stigma, not a blessing.

DASHAIN

Dashain is the most important festival to Nepalese Hindus. All offices and stores are closed for most of this 11-day celebration. Nepalese living away from their home village will go to great lengths to return home. All workers receive a bonus. Special foods are made and new clothes bought.

Dashain celebrates the victory of good over evil, represented by the victory of Goddess Durga (DUR-gah) over the demon Mahisasura (mah-hee-sah-SOO-rah), who terrorized the earth in the form of a huge water buffalo. Durga, the wife of Shiva, is often illustrated riding a tiger or a lion, her arms filled with the weapons she used to defeat Mahisasura, who lies prostrate at her feet.

The first day of *Dashain* is called *Ghatasthapana*, which literally means pot establishing. Each household plants seeds of grain. By the 10th day the seeds will have grown. This sacred grass is called *jamara*. On the ninth day, each household sacrifices an animal—a fowl, sheep, goat, or water buffalo— by slitting its throat or beheading it with a large *khukuri*. The blood from the animal is dripped over vehicles to ensure Durga's protection for the coming year. The sacrifices are followed by a big feast.

The actual victory of Durga over the demon is celebrated on the 10th day. Everyone puts on new clothes and visits relatives and friends to exchange greetings and *tika*. On the 11th day the *jamara* is distributed to every member of the family by the head of the household. The *jamara* is placed on the head as a sign of blessing.

Once a year, the chariot of Raato Machendranath is paraded through the city of Patan. Believers rush forward to touch it and pray for good fortune.

RATO MACHHENDRANATH

Every year, starting in late April, the city of Patan celebrates its biggest festival in honor of God Rato (red) Machhendra. During the chariot pulling festival of the rain god the image of the god, painted red and decorated with jewels and flower garlands, is taken from his temple and placed in a wagon topped by a 40-foot (12.2-m) pointed structure covered with pine. The wagon is pulled slowly by more than a hundred men through the narrow streets of Patan, stopping for the night in every neighborhood to give people the chance to worship. It can take a month or more for the wagon to travel through the city. Often the wagon collides with houses and the wheels get stuck in gutters. Each neighborhood takes turns to feed and care for the men pulling the wagon. The Nepalese, largely a farming people, believe that Rato Machhendranath controls the monsoon rains.

Celebrations for the Losar Festival at the Boudhanath Stupa. Losar is the biggest and most crowded festival of the year. Masked dances are performed and long copper horns are sounded. There is procession in which lamas carry a picture of the Dalai Lama around the stupa.

BUDDHIST HOLIDAYS

LOSAR   The most important festival in the Himalayan area is *Losar*, or New Year's Day. It is a time for dressing up in new clothes, exchanging gifts, visiting family and friends, and eating and drinking to one's heart's content.

At Boudhanath near Kathmandu, big crowds string prayer flags from the stupa. A photo of the Dalai Lama, the spiritual leader of Tibetan Buddhists, is paraded through the crowd.

At the climax, an exact moment determined by astrologers, everyone hurls handfuls of *tsampa* (SAHM-pah) flour, made from roasted barley, into the air, then at each other. Groups of people form long lines, with arms over each other's shoulders, and dance in a slow shuffle.

BUDDHA JAYANTI (Buddha JYAIN-tee) On the full moon in April or early May, the birth of the Buddha is celebrated by Nepal's Buddhist community. People make pilgrimages to a monastery, where lamas hold special services. It is also a time for feasts and visiting friends and relatives. In Kathmandu, Swayambhu Temple is the center of the celebrations, with thousands of people climbing the 300 steep stairs that lead to the top to worship at the many shrines around the stupa.

Women splash water on themselves on Mother's Day. People from Kathmandu Valley and different parts of the country reached Matatirtha to remember their deceased mothers, taking a holy bath to gain some salvation.

FESTIVALS OF THE FAMILY AND HOME

DASHAIN and **BHAI TIKA** These are festivals that combine the worship of a god and a goddess with a celebration that strengthens family ties. The main purpose of several other festivals is to strengthen the ties between family and home; these festivals are celebrated mostly within the family.

MOTHER'S DAY In Nepal, Mother's Day or Matatirtha is called *Aamaa-ko mukh herne din*, literally "see mother's face day." All children, including those that have married and moved away (usually daughters), return home to visit their mothers. They present sweets, fruits, and other gifts to their mother and, as a sign of respect, bend down so that their forehead touches her feet. The mother blesses them by placing her hand on their forehead.

FATHER'S DAY Called *Buaa-ko mukh herne din*, Father's Day or Gokarna Aunsi is celebrated in much the same way as Mother's Day.

RAKSHA BANDHAN (RAHK-shyah BAHN-dhahn) Girls tie decorated yellow silk threads around their brothers' right wrist and give the *tika* as signs of sisterly affection and devotion. In return, their brothers give them gifts and promise to look after them all their life.

NAGA PANCHAMI (NAH-gah PAHN chyah-mee) Nepalese civilizations worshiped the *Nagas* or Serpent Kings. *Naga Panchami* is an ancient tradition and festival that literally translated means Festival of Snakes. Houses in Nepal are usually built from clay bricks or mud and rocks. During heavy monsoon rains, many of the houses collapse. Nepalese believe angry snake gods living in the ground beneath the house cause it to collapse. To keep the snake gods happy, on Naga Panchami, every family hangs a picture of the Serpent King and his retainers above the main door of the house. A bright red *tika* is placed on the Serpent King's forehead. They pray to the snakes and place offerings of milk, honey, curd, and rice outside the house.

A Nepali Hindu takes sacred thread from a Brahman during the *Janai Purnima* festival. *Janai Purnima*, known as the sacred thread festival is the time when Hindu men, especially the Brahmins and Chhetris perform their annual change of *Janai*, a yellow cotton string worn across the chest or tied around the wrist of the right hand. This is a complementary festival to *Raksha Bandhan*.

INTERNET LINKS

www.nepalhomepage.com/society/festivals/festivals.html

This website has information on Nepal, including a calendar of festivals with links to detailed information on each festival.

www.diwalifestival.org/

Website with information on Diwali, one of the biggest Hindu festivals.

www.hinduism.about.com/cs/godsgoddess/a/aa090903a.htm

Website with information on Hinduism, including link to the Living Goddess of Nepal, Kumari Devi, and the Indra Jatra festival.

FOOD

A bustling vegetable market in Kathmandu.

W HEN TWO NEPALESE MEET on the road, the first question they will ask is *"Bhat khanu bhaeyo?"* (bhaht khahn-noo bhye-yoh), literally meaning "have you eaten rice?" but it actually means "have you had your food?" This shows the importance Nepalese place on eating rice.

Often, Nepalese use the word *"khanaa"* (khahn-nah), meaning "food," when they are talking about *bhat*, or rice. Rice is the staple food, but in most of the country, rice is a luxury and a sign of wealth and status.

Female farmers with rain covers working at a rice nursery in Pokhara.

The food in Nepal is as diverse as the country. The geographic and cultural diversity in the country furnishes a wide variety of cuisines based on ethnicity, soil, and climate. Some foods are a combination of Chinese, Tibetan, and Indian traditional dishes. *Momo* are Tibetan dumplings with Indian spices and traditionally filled with buffalo meat. There are many variations on traditional dishes to allow for dietary preferences and restrictions. Many of the dishes, especially in the poorer regions of the country, are derived from the need to eat rather than any special culinary skills.

Women harvesting millet in the Himalayan fields. Later, the millet grains will be either ground to make flour or fermented to produce liquor.

Rice can only grow at altitudes of up to about 6,000 feet (1,829 m), and it needs plenty of water. Most of Nepal does not meet these conditions. In many places rice is transported to small villages carried on someone's back, raising its price so much that many people can only eat rice on special occasions.

Most Nepalese depend on other grains—wheat, corn, and millet at low and middle altitudes and barley and buckwheat at high altitudes. The grain is ground into flour by hand or at a mill, and then boiled into a thick paste or made into *roti* (ROH-tee), a bread.

Nutritious and tasty, the classic Nepalese meal is *dal bhat tarkari* (dahl bhaht tahr-KAH-ree)—lentil soup, rice, and curried vegetables. Lentils provide protein, rice is the carbohydrate, and vegetables provide vitamins and minerals. Neither meat nor eggs are part of the daily meal. Milk and curd are more common, but not served everyday in most homes. *Achaar* (ah-CHAHR), pickled vegetables, is a popular side dish.

FOOD CUSTOMS

Food is only eaten with the right hand—the "clean" hand. Nepalese wash their hands before and after they eat.

During a meal, Nepalese pour some lentil soup over a portion of rice. They mix the soup and rice using their right hand, form it into a bite-sized portion, and pop it into their mouth. Then they eat some of the vegetables, pickles, or other side dishes. To a Nepalese, *dal bhat tarkari* eaten with the hand tastes better than when eaten with a spoon.

All the food on a plate becomes *jutho* (JYOO-toh), or "contaminated," when even the tiniest piece of food has been eaten. To offer leftovers to another person is a huge insult. Any food not eaten is given to the animals. This taboo is not as strong with people living in the Himalayas.

Meals are eaten twice a day, in the mid-morning and in the evening before bedtime, with a simple snack in between. Hindus are forbidden by their religion from eating beef. Brahmins have many dietary restrictions. They should not eat chicken, duck, buffalo, onions, leeks, mushrooms, and tomatoes. All foods are classified as "hot" or "cold" based on their effect on the body. Mango is hot; yogurt is cold.

Water is usually drunk from a communal pitcher. If a person's mouth touches the pitcher, the pitcher becomes *jutho* and must be thrown away. People drink by pouring water into their open mouth and swallowing at the same time.

A Nepalese Thakali feast fit for a king. Most Nepalese eat this kind of meal only during feasts or other very special occassions.

Just before rice is placed on a plate, the plate is rinsed with water. A dry plate is considered unclean. Before serving rice, Nepalese throw a few grains of rice into the fire as an offering to the gods. Nepalese do not eat dessert. After a meal, they chew a piece of betel nut, clove, or cardamom.

EVERYDAY FOODS

Nepal's main vegetable is potato, which is found almost everywhere. Spinach and squash are also common. Vegetables such as onions and carrots are rare, except in major towns.

There are very few refrigerators and very few canned foods in Nepal. In rural areas, vegetables are cooked as soon as they are picked. In towns, people usually shop everyday, buying the necessary ingredients for the day's meal.

Meat is a rare treat, usually served on festive occasions. Goat is the most common type of meat. Before a goat is killed, families in the village decide how the meat will be divided.

Milk is an important source of protein. It is always boiled and served

Skilled spice vendors at the Nepal markets will blend various mixes for a tasty culinary creation.

hot. Yogurt is also very popular.

Curry spices are ground together fresh on a stone for each meal. Nepalese use any of the dozens of spices sold in the market—turmeric, cumin, coriander, cardamom, pepper, fennel, fenugreek, ginger, mustard seeds, cloves, cinnamon, and nutmeg—or homegrown spices.

FOOD IN THE HIMALAYAN REGION

The food of the Himalayan area is based on several staples. One of them is butter tea. After brewing Himalayan tea, Nepalese pour it into what looks like an old-fashioned butter churn. They add butter and salt and churn the tea thoroughly. They then pour the salty, buttery tea into a jug and place it by the fire. To a foreigner, the taste may seem strange at first, but it usually gets better with every cup and can become a pleasant addiction. Healthy and hearty, Himalayan tea is drunk throughout the day and is the first thing offered to any visitor.

Tsampa, roasted barley ground into flour, is another staple food. People place the flour in a cup and mix it with butter tea into a thick paste. *Tsampa* can be made into a thick stew by adding potatoes and meat and is also made into thick *roti* and fried in butter.

The other staple is potatoes, boiled or baked in burning coals. A big plate of potatoes is a meal in itself. People eat potatoes by dipping them in a plate of salt ground together with hot chilies.

Meat is sometimes eaten, as the dry, cold climate preserves it for months. Buddhists are allowed to eat meat, but are forbidden from killing any animals. Himalayan people often hire people from the Middle Hills to come and slaughter the animals for them.

With no refigeration, dried goods are a staple food in the Nepalese diet. This store sells many kinds of dried beans, lentils, vegetables, and fish.

THE NATIONAL DRINK

Tea is Nepal's national drink. In Nepal the choices of what to add to tea go far beyond sugar, milk, or lemon. Nepalese add whatever spices they have handy. Ginger, cloves, cinnamon, cinnamon leaves, and cardamom are common additions to the teapot. Nepalese like their tea sweet, spicy, and milky. If there is no sugar, a pinch of salt is added to each cup.

On cold winter mornings, Nepalese brew raw ginger or ground black pepper in their milk tea. It is hard to imagine a more suitable drink on a cold winter morning than the Nepalese-style hot, milky tea, spiced with pepper or ginger.

LIQUOR

It is illegal to make liquor in Nepal, but it is rare to find a house in Nepal, except for high-caste Hindus, that does not. There are two main types of homemade liquor—*raksi* (RAHK-see) and *chhang* (chahng).

Chhang is a fermented beer-like drink with a milky texture. Almost always made from rice, but sometimes also from barley, corn, rye, or millet, *chhang* is almost a meal in itself. The Sherpas like to drink it in the afternoons and evenings.

In the Middle Hills and the Himalayan area, tea and sugar may not be easily available, so the morning may start instead with a glass of warmed *raksi*. More common in the average household than *chhang*, *raksi* is a distilled drink made

Local women enjoying *chhang*, a popular rice beer in Nepal.

from any type of grain, but usually from millet. Some brews use potatoes. Water is added again after it has been distilled. It is usually drunk warm, and some butter and a few grains of roasted rice are sometimes added to give it more flavor.

Drinking is a social institution in Nepal. Nepalese usually drink liquor accompanied by a small plate of snacks—meat, if possible. Eating meals and drinking alcohol are done separately. The meal is not eaten until drinking is finished, which means the meal may be delayed until 10 or 11 at night. After eating, the evening is finished and everyone goes home or heads for bed.

A favorite drink in the east is *tongba* (TOON-bah). Fermented whole grain millet is placed in a pitcher, hot water is added, and the concoction is sipped through a bamboo straw. Water can be added two or three times, and one pitcher may last through hours of convesrsation.

One traditional way to determine if the liquor is strong enough is to dip one finger into the brew and then hold a lighted match to the finger. If the liquor bursts into flame, it is considered to be of sufficient strength.

A young Nepali boy holding a cob of corn. In some of the outskirts of Nepal, food can sometimes be scarce and susceptible to variations in harvest.

INTERNET LINKS

www.food-nepal.com/recipe/R008.htm

This website is dedicated to Nepali recipes that are listed by Nepali and English names. It also has a restaurant guide.

www.ecs.com.np/index.php

This website is an online magazine, with links to information on living in Nepal. In the features section there is an article entitled "Bhaat Khanu Bhayo?" about food and it includes images and recipes.

www.explorenepal.com/recipe/

This website includes an introduction to Nepalese cuisine and has many links to individual traditional recipes.

DAL BHAT (LENTIL SOUP)

This recipe makes 6 to 8 servings.

1 cup masoor lentils*

3 to 4 cups (750 ml to 1L) water

½ teaspoon (2.5 ml) turmeric

pinch of salt

1 stick cinnamon

2 cloves garlic

1 small tomato

1 small onion

2 tablespoons (30 ml) oil

½ teaspoon (2.5 ml) ground cumin

½ teaspoon (2.5 ml) ground coriander

Yogurt (optional)

Wash lentils several times, removing any skins that come off. After draining the water away a final time, put lentils in a heavy pot with 3 cups of water and bring to a boil. Add turmeric, 1/4 teaspoon salt, and cinnamon. Partially cover, turn down heat to a simmer, and cook for one more hour. Stir occasionally and add more water if needed. As the lentils cook, mince the garlic and chop the tomato and onion. Heat the oil in a frying pan and add garlic and onion. Cook onion until transparent and add cumin and coriander. After a few minutes, add salt to taste. Then add tomato. Stir and cook. Try and time it so that this mixture is cooked as the lentils become soupy. Add the tomato mixture to the lentil soup and stir. Add more water and salt to taste. Serve over 4 cups cooked long-grain rice. A bit of yogurt is sometimes added at the end as a special flavoring.

Masoor lentils are salmon pink in color when dry, but turn yellow when cooked. If masoor lentils are not available, they may be replaced with plain lentils.

CHIYA (NEPALI MILK TEA)

This recipe makes 6 cups of tea.

3 cups (750 ml) milk

4 cloves

4 cardamom pods

4 teaspoons (20 ml) sugar

2 cinnamon sticks

3 cups (750 ml) water

4 teaspoons (20 ml) black tea leaves

Pour milk into a saucepan. Add cloves, cardamom pods, sugar, and cinnamon sticks. Heat milk until it comes to a boil. Let the milk simmer for a while, being careful not to burn it. In a kettle, bring water to a boil. Remove from heat and add tea leaves. Let sit for about 3 minutes. Carefully strain the hot milk into the tea. Gently heat for a few minutes. Do not boil, as this will make the tea bitter. Strain into tea cups and enjoy. Add more sugar if necessary. If sugar is unavailable, Nepalese sometimes add salt, pepper, or ginger to their *chiya*.

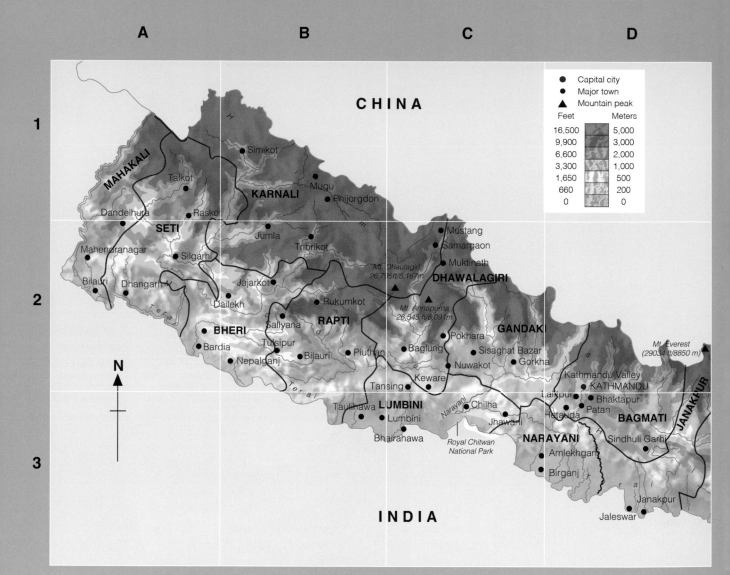

A   **B**   **C**   **D**

1

CHINA

● Simikot

KARNALI

Mugu ●
● Phijorgdon

MAHAKALI

● Talkot

Dandelhura ●   ● Raskot
SETI   Jumla ●
● Silgarhi   Tribrikot ●

● Mustang
● Samargaon
● Muktinath

Mt. Dhaulagiri
26,795ft/8,167m   DHAWALAGIRI

2

Mahendranagar ●

Bilauri ●   Dhangarhi ●
● Dailekh

Jajarkot ●

Rukumkot ●

● Sallyana
BHERI

Tulsipur ●
Bardia ●
Nepalganj ●   Bijauri ●   Piuthan ●

RAPTI

Mt. Annapurna
26,545 ft/8,091m

Baglung ●   ● Pokhara

● Sisaghat Bazar   GANDAKI
Nuwakot ●   ● Gorkha

Keware ●

Mt. Everest
(29034 ft/8850 m)

Kathmandu Valley
● KATHMANDU

Lalitpur ●   ● Bhaktapur
● Patan
Hetauda ●

Tansing ●

Taulihawa ●   LUMBINI
● Lumbini

● Bhairahawa

Narayani

● Chilha

Jhawani ●

Royal Chitwan
National Park

NARAYANI

BAGMATI

● Sindhuli Garhi

JANAKPUR

3

Amlekhganj ●

Birganj ●

● Janakpur

Jaleswar ●

INDIA

Legend:
● Capital city
● Major town
▲ Mountain peak

Feet	Meters
16,500	5,000
9,900	3,000
6,600	2,000
3,300	1,000
1,650	500
660	200
0	0

N

E

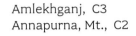

TIBET

SAGARMATHA

KOSI

Taplejung

Khotang

Dhankuta

Tribeni

Ilam

Dharan

MECHI

Udaipur
Garhi

Rajbiraj

Biratnagar

ECONOMIC NEPAL

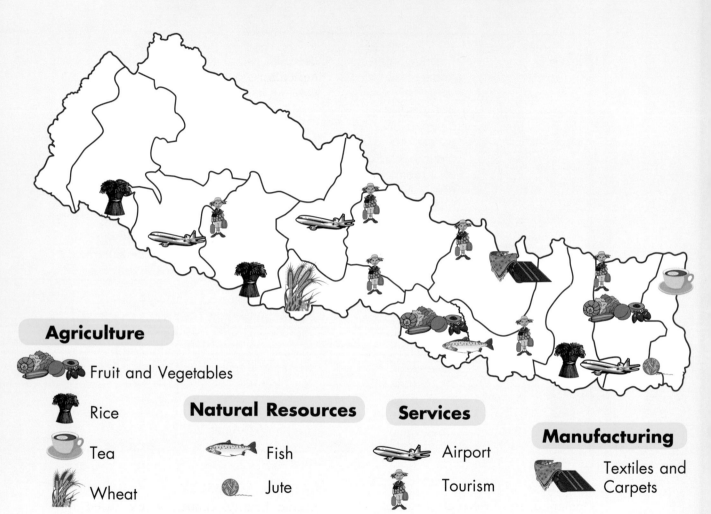

Agriculture

- Fruit and Vegetables
- Rice
- Tea
- Wheat

Natural Resources

- Fish
- Jute

Services

- Airport
- Tourism

Manufacturing

- Textiles and Carpets

ABOUT THE ECONOMY

OVERVIEW

Nepal is one of the least developed countries in the world. Agriculture is an important part of the economy. More than 75 percent of the people are farmers, but they produce barely enough to survive. Over 25 percent of Nepalese live below the poverty line. The textile and carpet industries and tourism are important activities, but the money made is used to pay for goods needed to support these industries. Nepal has great potential to exploit its potential in hydropower but political instability hampers foreign investment. It's landlocked geographic location, civil strife and labor unrest, and susceptibility to natural disaster, are further challenges to economic growth.

GROSS DOMESTIC PRODUCT (GDP)

$41.22 billion
Per capita: $1,300 (2012 estimate)

GDP GROWTH RATE

4.6 percent (2012 estimate)

CURRENCY

1 Indian rupee = 1.6 Nepalese rupees
1 Nepali rupee (NPR) = 100 paisa
Notes: 1, 2, 5, 10, 20, 50, 100, 500, 1,000
Coins: 1, 5, 10, 25, 50 paisa, 1 rupee
USD 1 = 97.8 NPR (October 2013)

GDP SECTORS

Agriculture 38.1 percent, industry 15.3 percent, services 46.6 percent

INFLATION RATE

9.5 percent (2012 estimate)

POPULATION

30,430,267 (2012 estimate)

WORKFORCE

18 million (2009 estimate)

UNEMPLOYMENT

46 percent (2008 estimate)

POPULATION BELOW POVERTY LINE

25.2 percent (2011 estimate)

EXTERNAL DEBT

$3.96 billion (2011 estimate)

AGRICULTURAL PRODUCTS

Corn, potatoes, pulses, rice, sugarcane, wheat, jute, root crops, milk, and water buffalo meat

NATURAL RESOURCES

Scenic beauty, timber, water (used for hydroelectric power), and small amounts of cobalt, copper, iron ore, lignite, and quartz

MAJOR EXPORTS

Carpets, grains, jute and leather goods, and textiles (mainly pashmina shawls)

MAJOR IMPORTS

Electrical goods, medicine, gold, equipment and machinery, and petroleum products

CULTURAL NEPAL

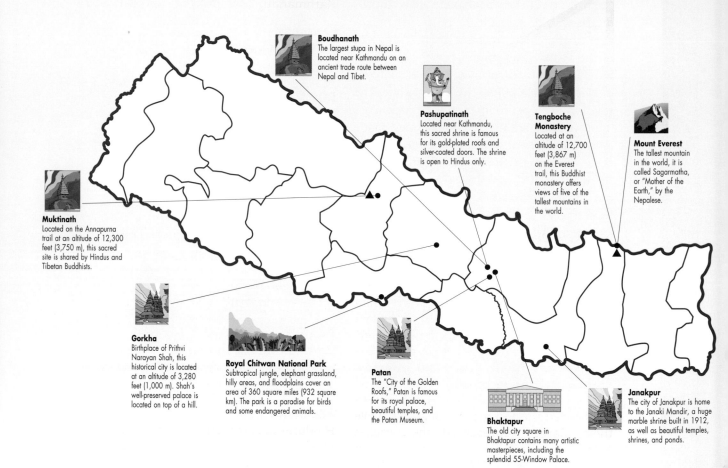

Boudhanath
The largest stupa in Nepal is located near Kathmandu on an ancient trade route between Nepal and Tibet.

Pashupatinath
Located near Kathmandu, this sacred shrine is famous for its gold-plated roofs and silver-coated doors. The shrine is open to Hindus only.

Tengboche Monastery
Located at an altitude of 12,700 feet (3,867 m) on the Everest trail, this Buddhist monastery offers views of five of the tallest mountains in the world.

Mount Everest
The tallest mountain in the world, it is called Sagarmatha, or "Mother of the Earth," by the Nepalese.

Muktinath
Located on the Annapurna trail at an altitude of 12,300 feet (3,750 m), this sacred site is shared by Hindus and Tibetan Buddhists.

Gorkha
Birthplace of Prithvi Narayan Shah, this historical city is located at an altitude of 3,280 feet (1,000 m). Shah's well-preserved palace is located on top of a hill.

Royal Chitwan National Park
Subtropical jungle, elephant grassland, hilly areas, and floodplains cover an area of 360 square miles (932 square km). The park is a paradise for birds and some endangered animals.

Patan
The "City of the Golden Roofs," Patan is famous for its royal palace, beautiful temples, and the Patan Museum.

Bhaktapur
The old city square in Bhaktapur contains many artistic masterpieces, including the splendid 55-Window Palace.

Janakpur
The city of Janakpur is home to the Janaki Mandir, a huge marble shrine built in 1912, as well as beautiful temples, shrines, and ponds.

ABOUT THE CULTURE

OFFICIAL NAME
Kingdom of Nepal

NATIONAL FLAG
Two red overlapping right triangles with a blue border. The upper triangle is smaller and contains a stylized white crescent moon; the lower triangle contains a white 12-pointed sun. The color red represents the rhododendron (Nepal's national flower) and is a sign of victory and bravery, the blue border signifies peace and harmony; the two right triangles are a combination of two single pennons that originally symbolized the Himalaya Mountains while their charges represented the families of the king and the prime minister, but today they are understood to denote Hinduism and Buddhism, the country's two main religions; the moon represents the serenity of the Nepalese people and the shade and cool weather in the Himalayas, while the sun depicts the heat and higher temperatures of the lower parts; the moon and the sun are also said to express the hope that the nation will endure as long as these heavenly bodies.

CAPITAL
Kathmandu

LAND AREA
56,827 square miles (147,181 square km)
Nepal has no sea access.

ADMINISTRATIVE DIVISIONS
14 zones (*anchal*); Bagmati, Bheri, Dhawalagiri, Gandaki, Janakpur, Karnali, Kosi, Lumbini, Mahakali, Mechi, Narayani, Rapti, Sagarmatha, Seti

LIFE EXPECTANCY
66.9 years (2013 estimate)

INFANT MORTALITY RATE
41.7 deaths/1,000 live births (2013 estimate)

ETHNIC GROUPS
Hindus: Brahmins (priests), Chhetris (warriors), Vaisyas (merchants and farmers), and Sudras (artisans); Newar: Kathmandu's indigenous people; Hill Groups: Gurung, Limbu, Magar, Sherpa, Tamang, Tharu, and Rai

RELIGIONS
Hindu: 80.6 percent; Buddhist: 10.7 percent; Muslim: 4.4 percent; Kirant: 3.6 percent; Other: 0.9 percent

MAJOR LANGUAGES
Nepali (official), Maithali, Bhojpuri, Tharu (Dagaura/Rana), Tamang, Newar, Magar, Awadhi

LITERACY RATE
57.4 percent of adults more than 15 years old can read and write (2011 estimate)

TIMELINE

IN NEPAL	IN THE WORLD

IN NEPAL

Seventh and sixth century B.C.
The Kiranti settle in the eastern hills and the Kathmandu Valley. Buddha is born in Lumbini.

A.D. 200
The Licchavi from northern India overthrow the Kiranti and establish a sophisticated kingdom.

879
The Thakuri overthrow the Licchavi; general decline for three centuries.

1200
The Malla Dynasty rises in Bhaktapur and spreads to other cities in the Kathmandu Valley; five centuries of great cultural advancement follow.

1364
Muslim raiders from Bengal take over Kathmandu Valley.

1482
Yaksha Malla dies; the kingdom is divided among his three sons.

1768
After 25 years of fighting, Gurkha ruler Prithvi Narayan Shah captures and unifies Kathmandu Valley.

1775
Prithvi Narayan dies; his successors expand the kingdom east and west.

1814
Nepal comes into conflict with the British East India Company; Anglo-Nepalese War.

1816
War with Great Britain ends with the Treaty of Seaguli that establishes Nepal's boundaries.

1846
Decades of court intrigue lead to Kot Massacre. Jang Bahadur Rana seizes power, sets up a ruling dynasty that lasts for a century and cuts off the country from the outside world.

1857
Nepalese troops assist the British in the Great Mutiny; Great Britain returns lands in the Terai.

1950
Nepali Congress Party leads revolts and King Tribhuvan dismisses the Rana prime minister.

1953
Edmund Hillary and Tenzing Norgay become the first climbers to reach the summit of Mount Everest.

1959
Nepali Congress Party wins the first free elections; B.P. Koirala becomes prime minister. Multiparty constitution adopted.

1960
King Mahendra seizes control and suspends parliament.

1972
King Mahendra dies and is succeeded by Birendra.

1990
King calls for elections after violent protests.

1991
Nepali Congress Party wins first democratic elections and G.P. Koirala becomes prime minister.

IN THE WORLD

1206–1368
Genghis Khan unifies the Mongols and starts conquest of the world. At its height, the Mongol Empire under Kublai Khan stretches from China to Persia and parts of Europe and Russia.

1789–99
The French Revolution

1914
World War I begins.

1939
World War II begins.

IN NEPAL	IN THE WORLD
1996	
Maoists in Western Nepal start violent attacks that last for more than a decade.	
1997	**1997**
Prime Minister Sher Bahadur Deuba loses no-confidence vote leading to a period of increased instability.	Hong Kong is returned to China.
2000	
G.P. Koirala returns as prime minister heading the ninth government in 10 years.	
2001	
Crown Prince Dipendra kills most of the royal family, then himself; King Birendra's brother, Gyanendra, becomes king; Maoists end truce with government and launch attacks on army and police posts.	
2002	
Parliament dissolved and new elections called. Sher Bahadur Deuba heads interim government. King Gyanendra dismisses Deuba and puts off elections.	
2003	**2003**
Rebels call off peace talks and violence escalates between activists and police.	War in Iraq begins.
2004	**2004**
Street protestors demand a return to democracy. Royalist Prime Minister Surya Bahadur Thapa quits.	Eleven Asian countries are hit by giant tsunami, killing at least 225,000 people.
2005	**2005**
King Gyanendra assumes direct control, dismisses the government, and declares a state of emergency. Maoist rebels and main opposition parties agree on a program intended to restore democracy.	Hurricane Katrina devastates the Gulf Coast of the United States.
2006	
King Gyanendra reinstates parliament. Government and Maoists sign the Comprehensive Peace Agreement.	
2007	
Under the terms of a temporary constitution Maoist leaders enter parliament. Three bombs detonated in Kathmandu and Maoists quit the interim government demanding that the monarchy be scrapped. Maoists agree to rejoin government after parliament approves the abolition of the monarchy.	
2008	**2008**
Nepal becomes a republic. Maoist ministers resign after disagreement over who should be the next head of state. Ram Baran Yadav becomes Nepal's first president. Maoist leader Prachanda forms coalition government, with Nepali Congress going into opposition.	Earthquake in Sichuan, China, kills 67,000 people.
2009	**2009**
Prime Minister Prachanda resigns over a row with President Yadav. Veteran Communist leader Madhav Kumar Nepal is named new prime minister.	Outbreak of flu virus H1N1 around the world.
2010	
Prime Minister Madhav Kumar resigns under Maoist pressure.	
2011	**2011**
Constituent Assembly fails to meet deadline for drawing up a constitution. Prime Minister Jhalanath Khanal resigns, Maoist party's Baburam Bhattari is elected as prime minister by the parliament.	Twin earthquake and tsunami disasters strike northeast Japan, leaving more than 14,000 dead and thousands more missing.
2012	
Three political parties resign from government over failure to agree on a new constitution, Prime Minister Bhattari calls for elections in November which are postponed.	

GLOSSARY

asylum
Refuge provided by a country to people fleeing political persecution.

bhaat (bhaht)
Cooked rice.

biogas
Gas fuel obtained from decaying organic matter such as sewage and plant crops.

chiya (chye)
Nepali aromatic tea, made with milk and spices.

dal (dahl)
A thick lentil soup, served at almost every Nepali meal.

hierarchy
A system that places people or things one above the other.

khukuri (KHOO-koo-ree)
Nepali knife characterized by a curved blade and considered a national symbol.

Mahabharata
One of the two great Hindu epics, it recounts the heroic struggle of five brothers against their 100 evil cousins (see *Ramayana*).

monsoon
A season marked by heavy rains caused by southwesterly winds in India and Southeast Asia.

namaste (neh-MEHS-tay)
The traditional greeting and farewell, spoken with hands clasped together.

prasad (prah-SAHD)
The blessing, usually in the form of food and flowers, received after finishing a puja.

puja (POO-jah)
The act of worshiping a Hindu deity.

Ramayana
The other great Hindu epic, it recounts the adventures of the great hero Ram.

stupa
A traditional Buddhist structure; a hemispheric mound topped with a spire.

thangka (TAHNG-kah)
Tibetan paintings with Buddhist themes, usually done on small- or medium-sized paper.

tika (TEE-kah)
A mark of blessing on the forehead, symbolizing the third eye of wisdom and inner knowledge, usually made with red powder.

Vedas
The Hindu scriptures dating back to 2000 B.C.

FOR FURTHER INFORMATION

BOOKS

Kipp, Eva. *Bending Bamboo, Changing Winds.* Kathmandu: Pilgrims Book House, 2006.

Mayhew, Bradley. *Lonely Planet Nepal (Country Guide).* Melbourne: Lonely Planet, 2012.

McConnachie, James. *The Rough Guide to Nepal.* New York: Rough Guides Publishing, 2012.

Stephenson, Joanne. *Decision: The Story of Kumar, a Young Gurung Boy.* Varanasi: Pilgrims Publishing, 2002.

Tenzing Norgay, Jamling. *Touching My Father's Soul: A Sherpa's Journey to the Top of Everest.* San Francisco: HarperCollins, 2001.

DVDS/FILMS

Everest. Miramax, 1999.

National Geographic — Everest 50 Years on the Mountain. National Geographic, 2003.

Kathmandu. Travel. Video Store, 2007.

MUSIC

Air Mail Music: Himalaya & Nepal. Boulogne, France : PlayaSound, 2000.

Band of the Brigade of Gurkhas. *Namaste (The Music of Nepal).* Indie Europe-Zoom Records, 2009.

Folksongs & Sacred Music From Nepal. West Sussex, United Kingdom: Arc Music, 1999.

BIBLIOGRAPHY

BOOKS

Anderson, Mary M. *Festivals of Nepal.* New Delhi, India: Rupa & Co., 1988.

Burbank, John. *Culture Shock! Nepal.* Singapore: Times Editions, 2000.

Connell, Monica. *Against a Peacock Sky.* New York: Penguin Books, 1991.

Hutt, Michael. *Himalayan Voices: An Introduction to Modern Nepali Literature.* Berkeley: University of California Press, 1993.

Mackenzie, Vicki. *Reincarnation: The Boy Lama.* Somerville: Wisdom Publishers, 1996.

Pye-Smith, Charlie. *Travels in Nepal.* Worthing, England: Littlehampton Book Services, 1988.

Taylor, Irene. *Buddhas in Disguise: Deaf People of Nepal.* San Diego: Dawn Sign Press, 1997.

WEBSITES

Central Intelligence Agency World Factbook (select Nepal from the country list). www.cia.gov/library/publications/the-world-factbook/

Country Reports (select Nepal from the country list). www.countryreports.org

Lonely Planet World Guide (select destination region, Asia, and destination country, Nepal). www.lonelyplanet.com/destinations

National Geographic Maps of Nepal. www.nationalgeographic.com/mapmachine

Nepal's newspapers and magazines. www.nepalnews.com

INDEX

INDEX